Dear Pat,

I pray this book will help you to abound in love for Him more + more in knowledge!

God bless,

Why God Is So Amazing!

30 DAYS TO A BETTER UNDERSTANDING OF GOD

David Tue

Consecration Press
NEW PORT RICHEY, FL

Consecration Press
9119 Ridge Road
Suite 11
New Port Richey, FL 34654
Website: http://www.davidtue.com
Email: david@davidtue.com

Ordering Information:
Quantity sales. Special discounts are available on quantity purchases by corporations, associations, and others. For details, contact the "Special Sales Department" at the address above.

Why God Is So Amazing / David Tue. —1st ed.
ISBN 978-0-9984114-0-8

Contents

To my Lord God - Holy, Immutable, All-Knowing and All-Powerful - who knows my sins are as numerous as the hairs on my head and yet has freely given His Son and adopted me as His child at great cost.

And to my wife, Jackie, who gave me the idea for this book and encouraged me throughout its creation. Thanks for your faith in me.

Your thoughts of God are too human

—MARTIN LUTHER IN HIS LETTER TO ERASMUS

Introduction

What is the first word that comes to mind when you think about each of these following animals:

- Sheep
- Tiger
- Lion
- Penguin
- Fish

What you thought about for each animal is called an attribute. An attribute is a characteristic that makes something what it is. All sheep have wool. If it doesn't, it's not a sheep. Therefore, having wool is an attribute of sheep. All fish swim. If it doesn't swim, it's not a fish. Tigers must have stripes. No stripes, no tiger. Hence, an attribute is a characteristic that the subject must have. If it doesn't have the attribute, then it isn't what we think it is. The definition of an attribute is "An inherent characteristic."

Often, we can know what something is by a single attribute. An example would be sheep and wool. In other cases, we need to know multiple attributes to recognize something. For example, a lion's attributes are its strength, sharp teeth, speed, and color. We use attributes to categorize things and understand them better.

What is it that makes a duck a bird? Ducks have bills, but not every bird has a bill; many have beaks. Ducks have webbed feet but most birds do not have webbing between their toes. Ducks swim in the water, but most birds spend their time in trees and cliffs. Though ducks fly, other birds, such as the penguin and ostrich do not. So what makes a duck a bird? Feathers! All birds have feathers and only birds have feathers. Also, all birds have wings, even if they cannot use them to fly. So anything with wings and feathers is a bird. This is what makes a duck a bird.

Attributes are Essential

Attributes are considered necessary parts. If a duck did not have feathers or wings, it would not be a bird. Cows are not birds because they don't have wings. Bats are not birds because they don't have feathers. In order to be a bird, an animal must have feathers and wings. Remove either of those things and it is no longer a bird.

This is true with God as well. The Westminster Catechism asks the question, "What is God?" While we are more used to hearing, "Who is God," by asking "What is God" we are specifically speaking about His attributes. The answer to "What is God" is a list of His attributes.

> *God is a Spirit, in and of himself infinite in being, glory, blessedness, and perfection; all-sufficient, eternal, unchangeable, incomprehensible, every where present, almighty, knowing all things, most wise, most holy, most just, most merciful and gracious, long-suffering, and abundant in goodness and truth. – The Longer Westminster Catechism, Question 7*

Though there are nineteen different attributes listed, others are not recorded in the Catechism. God is also Love, Triune, Faithful, Just and Righteous, to name a few. These lists give us an understanding of What God is. They describe the attributes that make up God. If one of these attributes were missing, God would cease to be God and would be something less than God. If God were Spirit, Infinite, Perfect and Eternal but not Unchangeable (Immutable), He would not be God. If He were Unchangeable, everywhere present (Omnipresent), almighty (Omnipotent), and most holy but did not know all things (Omniscient), He would not be God.

An animal that has wings but no feathers is not a bird. Therefore, a bat is not a bird. It might fly like a bird or act like a bird, but it falls short of being a bird. In the same way, God must have all the attributes of God to be fully God. If He were to be lacking just one of these attributes listed above, He would no longer be God.

Attributes Enable us to Know our Subject

The attributes of a subject enable us to know about it. Earlier, we listed some of the attributes of a lion: strength, sharp teeth, speed, and color. By knowing these attributes, we can learn much about the lion. The combination of the size and strength of a lion tells us that we wouldn't want to wrestle with it because it is bigger and stronger than we are. Knowing its speed, we wouldn't try to run from it because it can overtake us quickly. Realizing that its color enables it to cloak itself in its environment, we might be extra cautious when strolling through the African savanna. Hence, we know lions are dangerous and we ought to be aware and stay away.

By knowing the attributes of something, we understand how to interact with it. We shear sheep because of its wool. We wouldn't shear cows, though we would milk them. We wouldn't milk chickens, but we would check to see if they laid any eggs. By knowing the attributes of these animals, we know how to relate with them. We know what they are, what they can do and what we can expect from them.

However, there is a saying that goes, "A little knowledge is a dangerous thing." This is true with the attributes as well. My wife, Jackie, shared how she had at one time been fearful of people with severe autism. She knew some of the attributes such as the loud voices and the repetitive behavior. Then she went to school to become a teacher and learned about autism. Once she better understood the condition, she not only lost her fear but she loved those children and became a Special Education teacher.

All of this is true in our relationship with God as well. Often, Christians do not feel a need to study God's attributes because "I already know them." Pastors do not preach about God's attributes because "everyone already knows about them." However, without a complete picture of each of His attributes, we might be interacting incorrectly with Him and not even realize it. When we know, fully, "What God is," we will have a healthier relationship with Him. The more we know about His attributes, the better we will understand His ways and His thoughts.

About This Study

In this study, we will be looking at several of these attributes. The purpose of this study is to understand at a deeper level what these attributes mean and how they relate to God. For instance, we have often heard that God is Holy, but what does that actually mean? We know that God is immutable, but how does that affect the way I think about Him? Studying the attributes of God enables us to know Him properly.

The objective of this study is to help the Church return to a Biblical understanding of God. In the current church culture, we have turned our eyes from the Biblical account of God and have made Him into something different. As the world insists that God is Love and only Love, the church has taken that worldly mantra and made it our own. This is wrong. God is Love, but He is much more than that. If God is only Love and not all of these other attributes as well, then He is not God.

The methodology of this study is to concentrate on one attribute each week. Each attribute is presented in five sections. You will select any five days during the week to read a section. If studying this in a group, at the end of the week, the group will gather together to discuss what they have learned and to share any insights they have had.

Whether the study is read in a class or individually, the goal is to help us know God fully. My prayer is that you will be filled with a fear of the Lord, a reverence for our God and a deeper relationship with the One who knows you and longs to be known by you.

God bless you as you begin this journey.

CHAPTER 1

Holiness

Jackie and I have been married for 34 years. Most marriages struggle to survive that long in this day and in this culture. There was a time when 34 years was normal. Now, people are amazed that we have been together as long as we have. Many think we are outdated, living in the past and honoring an old-fashioned, bygone tradition. Others wonder what our secret is.

I think the reason our marriage has legs is because we know each other so well. I know when she is upset and she knows when I am frustrated. She knows my shortcomings (and there is a long list of those) and how to deal with me. I recognize what her facial expressions mean and react accordingly. We even understand each other when our conversation makes no sense.

"Did you see the…uh what do you call it…the, um, the squeeze thing around?" (As we get older, we seem to lose more vocabulary words every year…)

"I think it was next to the, uh, flesh cutter thing."

"Ah, yes! You're right!"

Jackie has found her tweezers next to her cuticle trimmer.

Yet, we don't know everything about each other, even after all these years. I still do things and say things that seem to surprise her and she still manages to do something that seems to come out of left field. In many ways, that's a good thing. We should never be so comfortable with each other that everything is old hat. Those surprises keep our marriage new and exciting.

However, if I don't know something about her that is important, that is crucial to who she is, we would have some very real problems. If I don't know her personality, her likes and dislikes, or her most important needs, our relationship is a farce. Then our relationship would be like living next door to someone for 34 years whom you have never really gotten to know. We would be strangers simply living at the same address.

Our knowledge of each other is foundational to having a real and thriving relationship.

The same is true regarding God.

Christians suffer a disturbing problem in this day. We call ourselves Christians and may even truly believe we are. We have said the sinner's prayer or gone forward for an altar call. We say we love Jesus and have accepted him as our Lord and Savior. Yet, if probed about our beliefs regarding God, we are hard-pressed to have solid answers. We don't really know what God is.

In the next several pages, we will look at the most crucial of all God's attributes: His Holiness. As important as it is, most of us do not understand it. What does it mean to be Holy? What does it mean that God is Holy? God's Holiness is essential to what God is and who God is. Therefore, we cannot truly be in a relationship with Him if we don't know His most elemental aspect.

Without understanding God's Holiness, we are strangers to Him, regardless of how many years we may have been living with Him. If we want to know more about our Amazing God, we must understand His Holiness.

Session 1 - What Does It Mean To Be "Holy"?

There are all kinds of Christians.

Some are super-spiritual. Every other phrase out of their mouth is "Praise God" or "Hallelujah." Conversations with these Christians go something like this:

"Hi Angel! Good morning."

"Brother David! Praise God! How are you this morning?"

"I'm good, thanks."

"Hallelujah!"

"How's it goin' with you?"

"Ah, I'm blessed and highly favored, praise God!"

"That's good. Well…I guess I gotta go…"

"Hallelujah, Praise God! It was a blessing to see you. Praise God. Tell Jackie I said God bless. Hallelujah."

Other Christians resemble their heathen neighbors. A conversation with them might sound like this:

"Hi Heath. Wonderful morning, isn't it?"

"Maybe for you. Wife's being a pain."

"Oh…sorry to hear it."

"Whoa! There goes Scarlet. Nice. Now she'd be a great wife. Just joking."

"Umm…so…Your wife's giving you a hard time? Do you want to talk about it?"

"Talking's for losers! Just joking. But I tell you, I never seem to make her happy. Always tellin' me to change this, or change that. I'm no different than everyone else. Sometimes I think I don't need to take this crud. 'Scuse my French….Hey! Did I tell you the one about the French guy with the frog in a bar?"

"I think so. Tell me again next time. I think I hear Jackie calling. Gotta go."

"Hey, tell her I said 'hi.' I'll see you guys at the picnic after church, right? It'll be fun! Don't want to miss that!"

Though Angel and Heath may not be our favorite Christians to hang around with, at least they are somewhat lovable. However, there is a Christian that is very difficult to love. This Christian is the legalistic Christian. A conversation with him might go like this:

"Good morning Lawrence."

"Good morning David. What are you up to?"

"I'm picking up Jackie to bring her to that new romance movie that just came out."

"You know, we're not supposed to support those Hollywood types."

"Yes, that's true. But what harm can come from this particular movie? After all, it's rated PG-13."

"PG-13! Oh No! You can't go to that! You might as well drive on the Sabbath or graze a woman's arm! You weren't planning to wear those clothes are you? The Bible is clear that we need to be Holy. Oh my, keep it up and you're on a fast train to Hell!"

Of course, I don't mean to offend by bringing up these different types of Christians. I am simply showing that our definition of living a holy life depends on our understanding of holiness. Each of these Christians has a distinct take on what holiness means. The first believes it means to act "spiritually" all the time. The second believes it doesn't matter as long as we receive Jesus as Lord and Savior. The last believes we must adhere strictly to all the rules.

Our objective in this study is to gain a proper understanding of holiness. By doing this, we will become better Christians, know God more completely and grow in our faith and relationship with Him.

EXERCISE 1

Q1: Our D____________ of H______ will determine what our living looks like.

Q2: Do you see yourself more like Angel, Heath or Lawrence? Why? Do you resemble someone else?

Q3: As you begin this course, what does a holy life look like to you? Write this down.

Q4: How does "living a holy life" and "who is God" relate to each other?

The Hebrew word "Kadosh"

"Kadosh" (kaw-doshe') is the Hebrew word translated "holy" in English. It is used to describe God. It is also used to describe people, priests, places, angels and the Sabbath day. When used in this way, it means "sacred" or "set apart."

'and you shall be to Me a kingdom of priests and a holy nation.' These are the words that you shall speak to the sons of Israel. – Exodus 19:6

God desired the nation of Israel to be holy. By this, He meant the Jewish nation would be set apart. They were not to be like the other nations. All the other nations disrespected life, but the Jewish nation would value it. All the other nations would treat women as property, but the Jewish nation would treat them as people. All the other nations would consider slaves as chattel, but the Jewish nation would view them as humans. All the other nations would perform child sacrifices, normalize homosexual activities, marry multiple wives, legalize prostitution, and worship many gods. The Jewish nation would refuse all of these. God calls them a peculiar people, not only because the Jews were to be a people of God's own possession, but also because they would be strange in the eyes of the rest of the world.

This is what it means to be holy.

The Greek Word "Hagios"

"Hagios" (hag'-ee-os) is the Greek word translated "holy" in English. It is used in much the same way as the Hebrew "kadosh." God is Hagios. People, the Temple and the Church are all called Hagios. As in the Old Testament, the New Testament term also means to be set apart. Holy people were to follow the ways of Christ and not the ways of the world. The ways of the world are seen as opposed to the ways of Christ.

So when one walks in the footsteps of Jesus, she is behaving in a way that is strange to the world. She is set apart from the world by her behavior and her actions. The Bible calls this fruit. It is strange fruit because it comes from another place than where the world looks for it. Many will ridicule her and persecute her. Some will admire her. A few will even desire what she has. In every case, she is set apart.

This is what it means to be holy.

To Be Holy is to Be Morally Perfect

Declan has many decisions he can make regarding the way he uses his time. Either he can visit some people in prison or he can go to the club. He can go to a mid-week Bible study or go to the gym to workout. He can visit the sick in the hospital or watch television.

Sophie has many choices she can make regarding the way she will react to her situations. She can either show grace to her neighbor or stop speaking to her. She can persevere in her marriage or she can split from him. She can refuse to gossip or she can spread some juicy news.

Declan and Sophie represent all of us as we choose on a daily basis whether we will follow the ways of the Bible or the ways of Man. God has called us to be Holy. We have been commanded to follow in the ways of Christ. We all have choices to make.

> *because it is written, "You shall be holy, for I am holy." – 1 Peter 1:16*
>
> *For you have been called for this purpose, since Christ also suffered for you, leaving you an example for you to follow in His steps – 1 Peter 2:21*

It is good to follow Christ's example for His ways are holy. Unfortunately, the ways of God oppose the ways of the world. This means that following Christ will deviate from the ways of the world. Our choices, like Declan's and Sophie's, depend on whether we want to be obedient to God or belong to the world. Know this: God is holy. God is good. Hence, God's ways are holy and good. When we are obedient, our walk will be holy and good. A holy life is an obedient life.

But Peter and the apostles answered, "We must obey God rather than men. – Acts 5:29

"If you love me, you will keep my commandments." – John 14:15

"Why do you call me 'Lord, Lord,' and not do what I tell you?" – Luke 6:46

Jesus knows when we are simply calling him "Lord" and when we actually treat Him as "Lord." There are many who call Him Lord, but few who follow his Lordship. Yet, the difference between a holy people and an unholy people is whether they follow the commands of God.

EXERCISE 2

Read Hebrews 12:14, James 2:26, 1 John 2:6, 1 John 3:9

Q1: A Holy Life is an O_______________ L_________.

Q2: The only way we will see the Lord is by living a H_______ L_______.

Q3: If we are abiding in Him, we are walking the same way J_______ w_______.

We are called to be holy. Yet, the best we can do falls short of the holiness of God. Only God is fully holy. Only God is completely separate. Only God is morally perfect. God requires that we be the holiest people possible, but if we are honest in our observations, we will recognize the chasm between our holiness and God's.

CHAPTER EXERCISE

"We cannot grasp the true meaning of the divine holiness by thinking of someone or something very pure and then raising the concept to the highest degree we are capable of. God's holiness is not simply the best we know infinitely bettered. We know nothing like the divine holiness. It stands apart, unique, unapproachable, incomprehensible, and unattainable." – A. W. Tozer, The Knowledge of the Holy

Activity: In the space below, copy Tozer's quote, pausing after each phrase to grasp fully his meaning.

Session 2 – The Sinlessness of God

As explained in Session 1, to be holy is to be morally perfect. When we speak of the moral perfection of God, we mean His sinlessness. God's moral perfection means that everything He does is morally good and nothing He does is morally wrong. This is a definition of sinlessness. All moral judgments must have a standard by which any action is judged. When that standard is man's, that standard will change.

Think about the society we live in today. Many of our cultural norms are different from those of other countries. These differences result in our disgust of the Chinese infanticide of female infants, of the wife beatings in Islamic countries and the bride burnings in India, Pakistan and Bangladesh. In turn, they are sickened by our gay marriage, abortions and sexual freedom. So who is right? If man uses his own standards, then both are right…and both are wrong. They cannot agree because they have different standards. There is no definitive right or wrong. With this understanding, we should not be surprised that many Muslims danced in the streets when the World Trade Center was destroyed. It was evil in our eyes but good in theirs. How can both be right?

If we continue down this path, we will come to a destination where no countries can coexist. Every culture has its own set of values and traditions and these will result in opposing moralities. Can this possibly be the truth? In a Godless culture, it is inevitable. However, once God enters the picture, everything changes. Since God is now over all, He can determine what is morally acceptable. Since God determines this, then it no longer matters whether we agree with it or not. Either way, God's way is the right way.

God is the King. He is a good King. Everything He does is right. Therefore, nothing He does is wrong. God is sinless.

The Moral Perfection of God

God is perfect in every way. Everything He does is morally right. We call this the moral perfection of God. While we agree with this, we wrestle with it when things don't go the way we think it should. We *intellectually* understand God is morally perfect, yet we struggle *emotionally* when we see evil in the world. How can a good, morally perfect God allow this evil in the world to exist? This question is the number one reason many people become atheists.

I cannot stress enough the importance of recognizing the difference between our intellect and our emotions. Our emotions always cloud our minds. We often make terrible decisions when we are in emotional states. If all our decisions and our beliefs are based on our emotions, we will find we have taken many wrong turns on the journey to truth.

Therefore, taking our emotions out of the equation, how do we explain the evil we find in the world residing alongside our morally perfect God? The answer is really rather simple. I will use the popular notion of the Butterfly Effect to illustrate. The Butterfly Effect says that a butterfly flapping its wings in China can cause a hurricane in Bermuda. The idea is that a small change somewhere can have a great effect somewhere else.

This is how our morally perfect God works. We cannot see the big picture. We are not omniscient and outside of time. Therefore, all we can see is what is displayed before us. However, since God can see the future and is able to determine the effects of evil, He is also able to ascertain when an action will result in the consummation of His perfect plan. When it does, He allows it to happen, even if we don't understand it. If it does not, He will intervene to set things right. In any case, He is the God who knows what is best, not for the moment, but for eternity. If we agree intellectually that God is omniscient and morally perfect, we can understand how He can coexist with evil.

> *And we know that God causes all things to work together for good to those who love God, to those who are called according to His purpose. – Romans 8:28*
>
> *Good and upright is the Lord;*
> *Therefore He instructs sinners in the way. – Psalm 25:8*
>
> *To declare that the Lord is upright;*
> *He is my rock, and there is no unrighteousness in Him. – Psalm 92:15*
>
> *And He said, "I Myself will make all My goodness pass before you, and will proclaim the name of the Lord before you; and I will be gracious to whom I will be gracious, and will show compassion on whom I will show compassion." – Exodus 33:19*

EXERCISE 1

Q1: When man creates the moral standards, those standards will inevitably C__________.

Q2: God determines what is M____________ A________________.

Q3: In order to understand evil in the world, we must separate our I_____________ from our E___________.

Q4: God knows the beginning from the end and causes A___ T________to work together for good.

The Sinlessness of Jesus

Jesus came to save sinners. So here's a quick logic problem for you: If the Savior is a sinner, can he save sinners? Of course not. Just as a dirty rag cannot clean but will only make things dirtier, a sinner cannot save sinners. Hence, logically speaking, Jesus must be sinless if He is to be the Savior of sinners. Is this what we learn in the Bible?

> *Which one of you convicts Me of sin? If I speak truth, why do you not believe Me? - John 8:46*

Jesus calls Himself sinless. He says, "Which one of you convicts Me of sin?" He is issuing a challenge. He is saying, "I know I have not sinned. I dare anyone to find even one time when I have sinned." Jesus knows He has never sinned and He calls attention to it here so that anyone who would think about His words would recognize the Truth of what He said.

> *He made Him who knew no sin to be sin on our behalf, so that we might become the righteousness of God in Him. – 2 Corinthians 5:21*

Paul knew Jesus never sinned. In his letter to the Church at Corinth, he shares the gospel to remind the brethren there of who Christ is. He is the one who never sinned and came to Earth so that He could take our place on the cross. Only the perfect lamb could be the Passover sacrifice. Even so, only the sinless Savior could be our sacrifice for the forgiveness of our sins. The proof of His sinlessness is the Father's acceptance of His blood. We call this the propitiation. Because the Father has accepted the sacrifice of His Son, we can now become the righteousness of God.

> *For we do not have a high priest who cannot sympathize with our weaknesses, but One who has been tempted in all things as we are, yet without sin. – Hebrews 4:15*
>
> *For it was fitting for us to have such a high priest, holy, innocent, undefiled, separated from sinners and exalted above the heavens; – Hebrews 7:26*
>
> *And having been made perfect, He became to all those who obey Him the source of eternal salvation, – Hebrews 5:9*

The writer of Hebrews also understands Jesus' sinlessness. Of all the writers of the New Testament, his letter has the most reminders of this fact. The writer compares Jesus as our High Priest to the human High Priest. His point is that there is no comparison. Why? Because Jesus was sinless.

He was not sinless due to a sheltered or protected life. As a man, Jesus was tempted in every way just as we are. Some claim Jesus was protected by God so that he would not sin. This is the same argument made by Satan regarding Job. At that time, Satan accused God of protecting Job so that nothing could touch him. God allowed Satan to do what he would against Job. This is true with Jesus as well. Satan tempted Jesus, not only in the desert, but throughout his life. Yet Jesus stood strong and never gave in to the temptations.

When we are first tempted, we are often able to reject the temptation. We give in to the temptation after it has been offered to us several times. If we can picture the path of a temptation, we would see it becoming stronger after each attempt. We usually give in at some point because the temptation becomes too strong for us to resist. Jesus never gave in. Therefore, we cannot imagine the strength of all the temptations that Jesus rejected. They must have been tremendously powerful. No one has felt the intensity of temptations as much as Jesus did because he never gave in to them. Since we've never experienced what Jesus did, we cannot empathize with him, but he can sympathize with us when we are tempted and fall. He knows how difficult it is to overcome temptation. Yet, Jesus did overcome them. He did not sin.

For you have been called for this purpose, since Christ also suffered for you, leaving you an example for you to follow in His steps, who committed no sin, nor was any deceit found in His mouth;
- 1 Peter 2:21-22

You know that He appeared in order to take away sins; and in Him there is no sin. – 1 John 3:5

Peter and John also understand the sinlessness of Christ. Peter teaches us that Jesus committed no sin. John tells us there is no sin in Him. The two great apostles agree that Jesus was the sinless savior. Hence, Jesus, Paul, the writer of Hebrews, Peter and John all agree that Jesus was sinless.

Charles Spurgeon said, "In holiness God is more clearly seen than in anything else, save in the Person of Christ Jesus the Lord, of whose life such holiness is but a repetition."

CHAPTER EXERCISE

Q1: Why is God the moral lawmaker? What does this tell you about God?

Q2: This chapter defined the part of Holiness that is Moral Perfection. What does this mean and why is this important?

Q3: Why is it important to understand that Jesus was morally perfect? What would it mean if He were not?

Q4: Explain why it is impossible for any one Person of the Godhead to be morally imperfect.

Session 3 - The Separateness Of God

When my family moved out to Long Island, I was five-years-old. The schools on Long Island were a bit harder than those in Queens. When it was time for me to be placed in a class, I don't think I did very well on the test. I was assigned to the class without many prodigies.

During lunch recess on my first day, I sat alone not knowing anyone. First graders aren't necessarily hospitable without having a good reason to be. After lunch was eaten, the entire class went outside to play. That's when the teasing started. It was time to make fun of the new kid. "The new kid ain't so smart." "Look at the puny new kid." And then, the oldie but goodie: "Chinese, Japanese, dirty knees, look at these!" The entire school, or so it seemed, was running around pulling at the corners of their eyes calling out, "I'm Chinese! I'm Chinese!"

Just as the tears began to fall, anger welled up inside of me. I did something out of character. I began screaming and chasing whoever was nearest me. It just so happened that one of the bigger kids was in the vicinity of my outrage. I don't know what actually happened, but I was somehow on top of him, karate chopping him with both hands (I guess I took the whole Chinese thing a bit too seriously). I received a bit of a scolding from the teacher but I never was teased again and the kid I "chopped up" became my first friend in that school.

As we come to this session on the separateness of God, I wanted to share that story to explain what separateness is not. I was certainly separated out. It wasn't because I was in the not-so-smart class. It wasn't because I was short. It wasn't because I had Chinese heritage. I simply was someone no one else knew. As others came to know me, I was accepted as one of them and was no longer separated out. My separateness was not due to anything about me and it didn't last long.

In contrast, God's separateness is fully about Him. He is nothing like us and we will never be the same as He. In this day, when the most spiritual people talk about God like He's one of their buddies, when love is His overriding principle in dealing with sin, when Hell has become an old-fashioned idea and His justice applies only to those who have committed the most heinous of crimes, His separateness has all but been forgotten. However, just because we don't see something doesn't mean it isn't there. It is time for the eyes of the Church to be opened. We need to remember the separateness of God.

God's Otherness

Holiness is God's overarching attribute. All of His other attributes originate from His Holiness. God's holiness is the rock from which all His other attributes pour forth. Our problem is, we have become so familiar with God that we have lost sight of His Holiness. We talk of His Love, His Grace, His Mercy, His Peace but we don't sing "Holy, Holy, Holy" like the Church of old. All of the teachings about God being our Father, about Jesus being our brother, about the Holy Spirit intimately living within us has resulted in our thinking of God as just another member of our family.

While much of this is good, even Biblical, we can go too far…and we have. We take for granted that He will always be there, in the same way we assume our parents are. We get angry with Him and scream at Him because we know He will let it slide, which is the way we might treat our spouse, children or siblings. I have heard from many Christians that, "It's OK to yell at God. He already knows how you feel. You're just being honest." These Christians epitomize our ignorance of His holiness. If we had even the slightest hint of understanding the holiness of God, we would never do these things.

Others try to grasp God's holiness by comparing it to something they know. Too many people think of God as someone who happens to be better than the greatest person. We need to recall the quote from Tozer: understanding God's holiness is not "thinking of someone or something very pure and then raising the concept to the highest degree we are capable of. God's holiness is not simply the best we know infinitely bettered."

Here is the proper way to think about Him: There is an essential difference between God and us.

We cannot make up for this by simply thinking bigger. God is something else. He is an "other." He is other than anything we have experienced or known. Not different, but other. I may be different from you in many ways, maybe even in every way. Yet I am not an "other" and neither are you. We are still the same, just different. Not with God. He might be the same as us in many ways and yet He is still an "other."

Sam Storms reminds us, "The holiness of God only secondarily refers to His moral purity, His righteousness of character. It primarily points to His infinite otherness. To say that God is holy is to say that He is transcendentally separate. Holiness is not one attribute among many. It is not like grace or power or knowledge or wrath. Everything about God is holy. Each attribute partakes of divine holiness."

"To whom would you liken Me
And make Me equal and compare Me,
That we would be alike? – Isaiah 46:5

"Remember the former things long past,
For I am God, and there is no other;
I am God, and there is no one like Me, - Isaiah 45:9

"These things you have done and I kept silence;
You thought that I was just like you;
I will reprove you and state the case in order before your eyes. – Psalm 50:21

EXERCISE 1

Q1: God's Holiness is not only about His M_______ P_________, but especially about His S____________________.

Q2: To be Holy is to be set apart. God's separateness is not simply that He is set apart but that He is "O_________."

Q3: Holiness is God's overarching A____________. Every other A__________________ is connected to and subservient to His Holiness.

Take the best person in the world. Remove all his or her flaws. Add in a collection of the best aspects of every other person ever. You still aren't close to having someone like God. Multiply that person by one hundred, one thousand, one billion, and God is still miles above. God is someone unlike anyone in Creation. He alone is God.

Understanding God's Holiness Leads to Worship

Considering God's otherness will lead us to worship Him. When we ponder His otherness, we will begin to see how far above us He is. He is not above us in distance but in value. He is higher than we can comprehend, deeper than we can understand, He is more than we can fathom, and He is of greater value than we can even think. We will come to these conclusions when we recognize His otherness.

We cannot fully grasp His otherness. It is why we cannot fully comprehend His holiness. Baker's Theological Dictionary of the Bible says, "The idea of holiness is at once understandable and elusive. Nevertheless, there is not a term equal to the fullness inherent in holiness. All of heaven's hosts, Israel and the church ascribe praise to a holy God because that idea sets Him apart from everything else." Just when we think we might understand His holiness, we realize it eludes us. This holiness causes all Creation to praise Him.

> *Who will not fear, O Lord, and glorify your name? For you alone are holy. All nations will come and worship you – Revelation 15:4*
>
> *And one called to another and said: "Holy, holy, holy is the Lord of hosts; the whole earth is full of his glory!" – Isaiah 6:3*
>
> *"There is none holy like the Lord; there is none besides you;" - 1 Samuel 2:2*
>
> *"Who is like you, O Lord, among the gods? Who is like you, majestic in holiness, awesome in glorious deeds, doing wonders? – Exodus 15:11*

Those who attempt to understand God's holiness respond in this manner: The cherubim cry out "Holy, Holy, Holy!" The nations will bow down and give Him worship! It is natural for us to worship God when we contemplate His holiness.

EXERCISE 2

Q1: The idea of God's holiness is at once U________________ and E____________.

Q2: When we begin to understand God's holiness and His otherness, W_________ will be all we can do.

Activity: Read Revelation 4-5. Count the number of times God/Jesus is worshipped.

Q3: In the song, "I Can Only Imagine," the singer questions whether he will "stand in your presence or to my knees will I fall?" Based on Revelation 4-5, what will he most probably do? Why?

Understanding God's Holiness Leads to Relationship

The god worshipped in every religion is considered holy. When adherents to these faiths come to understand what a holy god is, they typically begin to fear that god. The holy gods of the world's religions cause people to tremble. This was true in the time of Moses. It was true in the time of Jesus. It is still true today.

Yet, when the True God shows Himself holy, His people have a different reaction. We grow closer to Him. Our relationship with Him deepens. We do not fear Him. We worship Him. At first, we were unable to know Him due to our ignorance of His holiness. When we become aware of His holiness, we desire to know Him more, then we long to draw nearer to Him, which is followed by our impulse to worship Him, day and night, looking forward to the day when we fall on our knees in His presence before His throne, in Heaven where we will be forever with Him, being loved by Him and continuing to know His holiness more and more…

This attitude of the Christian towards God's holiness is as different from all other religions as chalk is from cheese. It is important that Christians regain their understanding of God's holiness before they end up like the followers of all other religions. Without the knowledge of God's holiness, Christians worship a false god.

CHAPTER EXERCISE

Q1: In other religions, a holy god is F_________.

Q2: In Christianity, we grow D_________ in R_________________________ with Him.

Q3: On a scale of 1 – 5, where 1 is, "I don't get God's holiness" and 5 is, "Every time I think about God, I begin to weep for joy and worship Him" where would you rate yourself? Why? Do you want to move up the scale? If so, what can you do to raise your awareness of His holiness?

Find a worship song or hymn that worships God's holiness. Play that song in the privacy of your prayer closet and worship Him as you pay attention to the words.

Session 4 - How God's Holiness Affects Us

So far in this lesson, we have learned what Holiness means. We have studied the aspects of Holiness: moral perfection and separateness. Up until now, our gaze has been invariably upon God. We have seen how the definition of Holiness applies to Him. We have discussed His sinlessness and His separateness, that He is altogether an "other" from anything in Creation. However, we have not discussed how this affects us. What does it mean to us that God is holy?

> *'For I am the LORD your God. Consecrate yourselves therefore, and be holy, for I am holy. – Leviticus 11:44*
>
> *'Thus you are to be holy to Me, for I the LORD am holy; and I have set you apart from the peoples to be Mine. – Leviticus 20:26*
>
> *because it is written, "YOU SHALL BE HOLY, FOR I AM HOLY." – 1 Peter 1:16*

The Bible gives us the answer in the Old and New Testaments. Since God is holy, we are called to be holy. We are called to be set apart and morally perfect. Let's see what that might look like.

Being Morally Perfect

Goodman is known to be a fine person. He is kind to his family. He helps his neighbors whenever they are in need. He spends time at the church and at the soup kitchen caring for the homeless and the hungry. Goodman tithes every week and makes good will offerings as well. He is well versed in the Bible and shares the gospel with others who haven't been as fortunate as he is when it comes to knowing Christ.

EXERCISE 1

What other behaviors come to mind when you think about being morally perfect. If you are studying as part of a group, stop here to brainstorm some behaviors you would add to Goodman's list. If you are studying on your own, write the behaviors that come to your mind in the space below.

You might be thinking, "Nobody's morally perfect! That's impossible." Good for you. You are correct; nobody can be holy like God is holy. Though God calls us to be holy as He is, He does not expect anyone will reach moral perfection. God knows we are not capable of this. He also knows that it is important that we try. He has not given us this command so that we will fail. He has given it to us so we have a goal. Our goal is to be holy as He is, even if we know we can never get there.

Yet, we can reach a level of holiness. We may not be able to become like God, but He has given us a measure of holiness. He gives us the portion that finite beings can handle. He expects us to live up to that potential. However, since the Fall, we are no longer able to reach that level of holiness. We first must be fundamentally changed. This happens when we receive His Son as our Lord and Savior. When we do, we are adopted by God as sons and daughters, called His own and become new creations. Only then can we reach the place of holiness demanded by our Father.

Notice the order: We receive Jesus as Lord; God adopts us into His family; we become new creatures; we grow in holiness. The order is important. Too often, men have gotten this wrong. They believe it goes: Be holy; Enter into Heaven. We cannot even attain holiness unless we first receive Jesus. This is out of order; it has been flipped around. God does not expect us to be holy so that we can enter into Heaven. He does expect those going into Heaven to be holy.

Being Separate

God calls us to separate ourselves from the world.

> *"Blessed are you when men hate you, and ostracize you, and insult you, and scorn your name as evil, for the sake of the Son of Man" – Luke 6:22.*
>
> *"They are not of the world, even as I am not of the world. – John 17:16*
>
> *Do not be bound together with unbelievers; for what partnership have righteousness and lawlessness, or what fellowship has light with darkness? Or what harmony has Christ with Belial, or what has a believer in common with an unbeliever? – 2 Corinthians 6:15*
>
> *"Therefore, COME OUT FROM THEIR MIDST AND BE SEPARATE," says the Lord. "AND DO NOT TOUCH WHAT IS UNCLEAN; And I will welcome you. – 2 Corinthians 6:17*

To be holy is to be separate. When something pure is exposed to something polluted, it becomes unclean. The sinful world is soiled to such an extent that to be a part of it is to corrupt oneself. Hence, holiness is separateness. It is being something “other” than everyone else. While God is fully “other” than all Creation, we can be somewhat “other” from the world. We can be separate from the world. However, separation from the world does not mean isolation from it.

EXERCISE 2

Think of ways that we can be separated from the world without being isolated from it. Example: Your co-workers are going to Hooters for lunch, so you join the accounting department at the diner.

Think of ways you can be an “other” in the world. Example: After work, you join your co-workers at the bar but order a cola.

Our "otherness" will be conspicuous in any environment where the world has snuck in. This may be in your workplace or in your neighborhood. It may also be in your family or in your church. When Jackie and I first came to know the Lord, we had been attending church for many years. Prior to our salvation, we were integral parts of a church family. We headed committees, led the Youth Group and joined mission trips.

When we were born again, we suddenly saw the world intertwined throughout everything the church was doing. The goal of evangelism was to gain numbers, not to save the lost. Mission was to help people in poor countries, not spread the gospel throughout the world. Tithing was to raise enough money to fix the roof, not to honor and worship God. We began to change our interaction with the church. We started to share the gospel. We began a new worship service. We created a team to reach the lost.

It was only a matter of time before our behavior began to be noticed. We had become "others." We started to hear whispers about "those God people." We took it as a badge of honor. What Christian wouldn't want to be called a God person? It reminded me of the brethren in Antioch. Their "otherness" caused the unbelievers to deride them and label them "Christian." What was meant as an indignity became a beloved title.

When people become uncomfortable, name calling is often the result. Sticks and stones. No big deal. But sometimes, it develops into persecution that is more serious. Take heart.

> *"If the world hates you, you know that it has hated Me before it hated you. If you were of the world, the world would love its own; but because you are not of the world, but I chose you out of the world, because of this the world hates you. Remember the word that I said to you, 'A slave is not greater than his master.' If they persecuted Me, they will also persecute you; - John 15:18-20*
>
> *Blessed are those who have been persecuted for the sake of righteousness, for theirs is the kingdom of heaven. – Matthew 5:10*
>
> *These things I have spoken to you, so that in Me you may have peace. In the world you have tribulation, but take courage; I have overcome the world. – John 16:33*
>
> *After you have suffered for a little while, the God of all grace, who called you to His eternal glory in Christ, will Himself perfect, confirm, strengthen and establish you. – 1 Peter 5:10*

Holiness in the Church

Jesus built His Church to be holy and blameless.

> *Christ also loved the church and gave Himself up for her, so that He might sanctify her, having cleansed her by the washing of water with the word, that He might present to Himself the church in all her glory, having no spot or wrinkle or any such thing; but that she would be holy and blameless. – Galatians 5:25-27*

Think about what Jesus gave up so that the Church could be holy and blameless. We will quickly conclude that the Church ought never to be like the world. However, as a child rebels against its parents, churches seem to be rebelling against Christ. We read earlier that we have been chosen out of the world, the world hates Jesus, and that the world loves its own. Hence, we would expect every church to be counter-cultural, to be hated by the culture and to be persecuted. To be sure, this is true in many cases.

Sadly, many other churches have abandoned this fight. They have determined they want to be loved by the world. The world has become a cauldron of sin: Divorce, gay marriage, adultery, abortion, cohabitation – the list goes on. In response, many churches have changed their own laws to allow this sinful behavior to exist within their four walls. They join in the post-Christian mindset in order to be less offensive to the world.

The Bible is clear regarding this. Jesus gave himself up for the Church so that she could be holy and blameless. When a church loses her holiness, it is time to close the doors. When a church is no longer blameless, the Christians should run out from it.

Instead, there is a proper way the Church is supposed to integrate into society. She is not to conform to society. She is to be "other." In the same way we as individuals can find ways to be separate and "other" without isolating, the church should also be separate and "other" without isolating.

Jesus told us we would have tribulation. He was not talking solely about individuals. He was speaking to the Church. If the church is purposely working to avoid tribulation, she is no longer the bride of Christ but the apostate church. With the number of churches that have relinquished their "otherness" and have embraced the ways of the world, even opposing the Word of God, we should not be surprised that the church has lost her power to transform the community.

Be holy as I am holy. God commands it. His Church must obey it. Otherwise, she is no longer His church and she should not be surprised when she hears:

I never knew you; depart from Me, you who practice lawlessness. – Matthew 7:23

CHAPTER EXERCISE

Q1: No one is M__________ P__________ but God still calls us to be H______ as He is H______.

Q2: S__________________ from the world does not mean I______________ from it.

Q3: Jesus died for the Church so she could be H______ and B__________________.

Recall one of the ideas you came up with in Exercise 2 to be an "other" in the world. Commit to doing this every day, or at every opportunity, for the next week.

Session 5 – Takeaways

The objective of this session is to summarize what we have learned throughout this study. Following are statements that reiterate lessons we have learned. Spend at least 30 seconds thinking about each one before going on to the next. During this time, meditate on the statement and make an effort to fully understand it, including imagining it by creating images in your mind. At 30 seconds per statement, the entire exercise will take 10 minutes. If you spend longer than 30 seconds on any or all of the statements, that's good. It means you have taken this lesson seriously and have a real desire to know the Holiness of God. Be still and know that He is God...

- Holiness consists of being morally perfect.
- Holiness consists of being completely separated.
- Holiness is God's overarching attribute. Every other attribute stems from this.
- God the Father is morally perfect. Jesus is morally perfect.
- For us to be holy, we must obey God.
- The morals of our society have become reprehensible during our lifetime.
- God allows evil in the world because it will somehow affect the outcome of eternity for the best.
- God is so separated from creation, He is considered an "other." Nothing is like Him in all creation.
- Even as we think of God as someone familiar, we dare not treat Him like one of the family.
- In light of His holiness, it is foolishness to be angry with God.
- Thinking of something holy and multiplying it to infinity won't help us know His holiness.
- We will never fully understand the "otherness" of God.
- When we contemplate God's holiness, we cannot help but worship Him.
- Though the holiness of God causes others to tremble, it draws us nearer to Him.
- God's holiness causes us to desire to be holy.
- We can never be fully holy as God is, but we can be as holy as Man can be.
- We are determined to live a separated life from the culture and society in which we live.
- The church is to be an "other" in the community and society where she is found.

Experiencing the Holiness of God

Imagine someone holy. Who comes to mind? Many people name one of the saints of the faith, such as Saint Francis of Assisi or Mother Teresa. Others consider their pastor holy. Still others recall a friend who has touched many lives for the good. When pressed to explain why they selected these particular people, they affirm the moral goodness of these saints. Yet, the moral goodness of all of these saints put together does not compare to the Holiness of God.

> *In the year of King Uzziah's death I saw the Lord sitting on a throne, lofty and exalted, with the train of His robe filling the temple. Seraphim stood above Him, each having six wings: with two he covered his face, and with two he covered his feet, and with two he flew. And one called out to another and said,*
>
> *"Holy, Holy, Holy, is the Lord of hosts,*
> *The whole earth is full of His glory."*
>
> *– Isaiah 6:1-3*

When Isaiah stood in the presence of God, he saw the majestic seraphim flying through the heavens, calling out to one another, "Holy, holy, holy is the Lord of hosts."

Imagine you are Isaiah.

You are in the throne room of God in heaven. To be clear, you are in heaven, the place every human desires to be forever. In heaven, you are in the place above every other place, the throne room of God. This is the most breath-taking, inspiring, overwhelming; formidable, intimidating, terrifying place in the world, in the universe, the spiritual realm, of all creation.

Seraphim are flying all about. In this most awesome of all places are the most magnificent creatures, the seraphim, a type of angel, so glorious, words can barely depict them. Isaiah tries but he can only sketch out a vignette of beings with six wings. While describing the seraphim is difficult, Isaiah has no problem telling us what they say, "Holy, holy, holy is the Lord of hosts."

The Lord – the one who is in charge, who gives out commands and orders.

Of hosts – all the armies of angels in heaven.

The Lord of hosts is NOT holy.

He is not holy, holy.

He is Holy, holy, holy.

Of course He is! Look and see what is before you!

The Lord. Sitting on a throne. He is not just a king. He is The King. The evidence for this is the place where His Throne resides. And the One who sits upon it is lofty, exalted, dignified and distinguished, majestic, grand and stately. The train of His robe fills the Temple, the Throne room, the Most Holy Place.

Can you do it? Can you imagine being Isaiah? Can you imagine being in that place, before the Lord of hosts? I can't. I just tried. It is beyond our grasp to conceive being before God. If you can, you still don't get how holy God is.

Isaiah, who actually did experience this, reacts by crumbling before God, crying out how cursed he is for being a man, a Jew, a human. Up to this moment, Isaiah recognized that humans were the most exalted of all creation and that the Jews were the most exalted of all humans. Yet, those things pale in the presence of the Holy God. Then, after the seraph touches his lips with a coal from the altar that stands before the throne of God, Isaiah is declared clean. His iniquities have been taken away. His sins have been forgiven. How does Isaiah respond to the mercy of this Holy God? He offers up his own life to go out to be God's mouthpiece, to do God's work, to be His minister. His life changes from that moment on.

CHAPTER EXERCISE

Q1: Isaiah tried to describe the Holy presence of God. What words would you use to describe this?

Q2: After reading the above chapter, would you say your understanding of God's holiness is greater, the same or less than it was prior to reading this? Why?

Q3: Isaiah saw how sinful he was in the presence of God's holiness. If you were transported into His presence right now, how do you think you would react?

CHAPTER 2

Immutability

Imagine the beach on a hot summer day. The cool breeze blows. The waves lap against the shore. The sand on your feet has just the right amount of rough and just the right amount of soft. You grab some sand with your toes. Nothing else has the same feeling. You walk the shore and let the waves caress your feet. You look out to the water and notice a piece of petrified wood floating back and forth, tossed in whatever direction the waves should go. On the shore, the birds walk beside you, sinking their bills into the sand, looking for whatever it is they eat.

Even with all this, the best part is when the sun rises or sets. Watching the sun ascend and descend across the horizon always results in colorful splashes of reds, oranges and yellows. If the clouds are right, the picture becomes grandiose. Since man has walked on the Earth, one of the most visible signs of God's handiwork displayed is in a sunset or sunrise on the beach.

Now what happens to that natural fireworks display when the skies are overcast or rain moves in? It disappears. Skip the photo shoot because there won't be any light show today. While we can look forward to another demonstration of God's creation on the next clear day, we have come to understand that each day is different. We trust we will see another beautiful sunrise at some point in the future. We know another stunning sunset is on its way before long. Although we don't know when, we have confidence in the reliability of the sun and sky to produce another spectacle soon.

While we don't have a problem with the changes in the weather or the beach conditions from day to day, how would we feel if God was like that? We don't really think about it much, but we expect God to be the same today as He was yesterday. In fact, we depend upon it.

I had a conversation with a Muslim once and I was struck by his idea of Allah. There seems to be contradictions in the Quran but apparently, Allah can change his mind if he chooses. To my thinking, this would be detrimental to one's ability to enter into heaven. If Allah changed his mind about the entrance fee, how is any law abiding Muslim to know whether he or she had paid enough to enter? What if Allah changed it by just a little? What if now a Muslim missed heaven by just that amount?

As if to validate my thoughts, I heard afterward a teaching from ex-Muslim-turned-Christian Ergun Caner. He said one of the most effective ways to reach a Muslim for Christ is to explain our assurance of salvation. While they are going to their graves unsure of their final destination, we go in peace and even in celebration because we *know* where we will be.

However, assurance of salvation is only valid because of God's Immutable Character. Immutability is the attribute of God which means He never changes. God is not like the weather. He is not stormy one day and bright shining the next. He is not like petrified wood floating to and fro wherever the waves go. He is not like Allah, who can change his mind and do something other than what he said he would. God never changes. He is unchangeable. He is immutable.

In this study, we will delve into what it means for God to be immutable. We will define this attribute, understand what it means and why it is important to us. When we have finished this study, we will have a better sense of what God is. This will enable us to know Him more and thereby draw us closer to Him.

Session 1 – Immutability Defined

It is rare to hear the term "Immutable" in a sermon. Most pastors and teachers don't spend too much time defining this attribute and explaining why it is so important. Yet important it is. The simple definition of "immutable" is "unchangeable." To say God is immutable means that He never changes.

> *"For I, the Lord, do not change; therefore you, O sons of Jacob, are not consumed. – Malachi 3:6*
>
> *"Of old You founded the earth,*
> *And the heavens are the work of Your hands.*
> *"Even they will perish, but You endure;*
> *And all of them will wear out like a garment;*
> *Like clothing You will change them and they will be changed.*
> *"But You are the same,*
> *And Your years will not come to an end. – Psalm 102:25-27*
>
> *Every good thing given and every perfect gift is from above, coming down from the Father of lights, with whom there is no variation or shifting shadow. – James 1:17*

According to Merriam-Webster's Dictionary, immutable means "unable to be changed." It isn't simply that something doesn't change. It is incapable of it. It cannot change even if change was desired. Merriam-Webster continues, "*Immutable* comes to us through Middle English from Latin *immutabilis,* meaning 'unable to change.' 'Immutabilis' was formed by combining the negative prefix *in-* with 'mutabilis,' which comes from the Latin verb *mutare* and means 'to change.'"

We are much more familiar with the English word, "mutate" and "mutation." We know these words from our childhood: we were taught that monkeys mutated into men and that men mutated into X-Men. In both of these fictional fairytales, we understand that something changed from one thing to another. Immutable and immutability mean the exact opposite. If something is immutable, it cannot change and never does.

When we say God is immutable, we are saying God never changes. As the verses quoted above state with no ambiguity, God does not change, He is the same forever, and there is no variation or shifting in His Person or His Word.

The Correlation of Change and Time

One of the traits of change is that it is measured over time. Without time, there is no way to know whether something has changed. Right now, you are reading this in English. You comprehend each word and sentence and they make sense to you. As far as you are concerned, the English you are reading hasn't changed. However, if we look back over the past 600 years, we realize how much the English language has changed.

> *Of old hast thou laid the foundation of the earth: and the heavens are the work of thy hands. They shall perish, but thou shalt endure: yea, all of them shall wax old like a garment; as a vesture shalt thou change them, and they shall be changed: But thou art the same, and thy years shall have no end. – Psalm 102:25-27 - King James Version 1611*

O Romeo, Romeo! wherefore art thou Romeo? – Shakespeare 1595

Whanne that Aprill with his shoures soote
The droghte of March hath perced to the rote. – Chaucer 1392

In the case of the English language, change has occurred over a long period. Sometimes we see change occur over short time spans. Caterpillars turn into butterflies in about four weeks. Spring turns to Fall in about six months. Beautiful infants turn into ugly monsters in about two years.

Whether a toddler in his Terrible Twos is a monster is beside the point (of course they aren't…not really). What is important is recognizing that for any change to occur, time is a necessary ingredient. If we could think abstractly for a moment, imagine time consisting of 1/1,000 of a second. Would it be possible for anything to change that quickly? How about 1/200,000 of a second (that's faster than light)? On the other hand, Darwinians believe that any change can happen if enough time passes. Life can spring up from nothing. DNA can accidently gain information that usually only comes from an intelligent mind, allowing one species to change into another more complex one. My point is that change can only occur over time and if we remove time from the equation, we stop the ability for change to happen.

This is what happens with God. It is literally impossible for God to change because God is outside Time. He created Time. He is not in His own Creation for He existed before He created anything, including Time. Since God is outside Time, He is not affected by it. Hence, without Time, there can be no change. By definition, God is immutable because He is the Eternal, Infinite, Creator God.

When we understand this, we can recognize how God can know the beginning from the end. He is separate from it. We see a small amount, even if we were to add together all the memories of everyone who has ever existed; we are still bound by Time. God is outside Time. He can see what has happened before anyone existed. He can see what will happen after everyone is gone. He can see everything in-between. This is why He calls Himself the Alpha and the Omega (these are the first and last letters of the Greek alphabet). Nothing is before Him and nothing after Him. This is because He is outside Time.

I like to use the analogy of a Director making a movie. He is not part of the movie but he can see everything that has happened on the film and can make cuts and changes that affect how the film turns out. Also, the Director can see what has happened at the beginning, at the end and in every place in-between. Although in the film, time has passed, the Director is able to see the beginning and the end at the same time. Although he is separate from the film, the Director is intimate with the film and cares for each character in the film. He gives his all for it, so much so that it seems as if the film is a part of him, even though it is not.

God is like this director. He is outside of the Time He has created. He cannot change since He is outside of Time. We are able to keep ourselves from false teachings when we understand God's immutability. There is a distortion of God's attribute of immutability called Process Theology. In this belief, God changes as time goes by. Now that we understand that God is not part of Time but separate from it, we can avoid this false teaching.

EXERCISE 1

Q1: Something that is Immutable is U____________ to C__________.

Q2: There can be no C______ without T_____.

Q3: God is O____________ of Time because He C___________ it.

Q4: The foundation of Process Theology is wrong because it misunderstands that God cannot C____________ since He is outside of T____________.

Imagine Time has stopped. What has happened to every living creature on the Earth? What has happened to every object out in space? If Time has stopped, can anything change? Stop reading here to take some time to imagine this and think deeply upon it.

The Great I AM

Moses lived in the desert for forty years. He had run away from Egypt and into the desert to hide from Pharaoh. Moses had killed an Egyptian and now Pharaoh was looking to kill him. For forty years, God worked in Moses, preparing him for the role he was to play. When the time came, God showed Himself to Moses in the form of a bush on fire that did not burn up. When Moses went in for a closer look, God spoke to him and gave him his new assignment: go back to Egypt and be His messenger. Moses, trying to find a way out of this mission, asked God for His Name. God responded with the Name by which He will be known for the rest of Eternity:

> *Then Moses said to God, "Behold, I am going to the sons of Israel, and I will say to them, 'The God of your fathers has sent me to you.' Now they may say to me, 'What is His name?' What shall I say to them?" God said to Moses, "I AM WHO I AM"; and He said, "Thus you shall say to the sons of Israel, 'I AM has sent me to you.'" God, furthermore, said to Moses, "Thus you shall say to the sons of Israel, 'The Lord, the God of your fathers, the God of Abraham, the God of Isaac, and the God of Jacob, has sent me to you.' This is My name forever, and this is My memorial-name to all generations. – Exodus 3:13-15*

God gives His Name as "I AM WHO I AM." God instructs Moses to say "I AM has sent me." What does it mean that God's Name is I AM WHO I AM?

To say, "I am" is to say, "I exist." But even more, it is to say, "I exist right now." "I am" is in the present tense. He exists at this moment. God doesn't call Himself, "I have always been." He doesn't say, "I will always be." This should make sense to us since we understand God to be outside of Time: He is not in the past nor is He in the future. He just "is." Time is irrelevant to Him. Every person who has ever lived in the past, or will ever live in the future, will experience Him at a moment in Time. Since God is outside of Time, we will all experience Him the exact same way. God does not have a past or future. He simply is.

God says that this is His name forever. Forever is a long time for us. For God, it doesn't stretch out the same way because He is not in Time. God says this is his memorial name to all generations. Every generation that will ever exist will experience God as "I AM." In the time of Moses, He was I AM. In the time of Jesus, He was I AM. Today, He is still I AM.

This is what it means for God to be immutable. He never changes. He is the same throughout all of Time. This is because He is outside of Time. Time doesn't affect Him. Simply, HE IS.

What About God Doesn't Change

We want to be precise when we say God is immutable. What about God doesn't change? In this study, we will break this up into two parts: God's Person and God's Will.

When we consider the immutability of His Person, we will be talking about His Nature, His Being, His Character, His Attributes. These are all different ways of saying the same thing. These are the aspects of God that deal with Who and What He is.

Additionally, we will study the immutability of His Will. We will point out His Purposes, His Promises, His Word. These pertain to the things He does.

> *"There is change round about Him, change in the relations of men to Him, but there is no change in His Being, His attributes, His purpose, His motives of action of His promises. – Louis Berkhof*

CHAPTER EXERCISE

Q1: The Name God calls Himself is __ _____.

Q2: God will be called I AM in every G_________________.

Q3: The two aspects of God which are immutable are His P_________ and His W______.

Copy James 1:17 below and memorize the verse:

Every good thing given and every perfect gift is from above, coming down from the Father of lights, with whom there is no variation or shifting shadow. – James 1:17

Session 2 – The Immutable Person of God

I will bet that at some time in the past, someone has made the same mistake for the umpteenth time and you said something like:

"People never change."

"People are so predictable."

"You can't teach an old dog new tricks."

These are sayings that are commonplace in our language and culture. Yet, if someone who has been doing something consistently in the past were to break out of that routine, we might say:

"Well, people change."

"People are so unpredictable."

"The only thing in life that never changes is change itself."

When we hold them up one to the other, we find our clichés and proverbs contradict each other. When it comes to understanding people, we have a habit of becoming confused. This is because every person is an individual and it is difficult to make general statements about people when there is such a variety. No two people are alike (another cliché!). Hence, some people will never change. Others never stay the same. Most people stubbornly remain the same in some areas of thought and life while bouncing from one place to the next in other areas. It's the fickle nature of people.

There is no fickleness with God. His nature will be the same always. God depicts Himself in the Old Testament the same way He describes Himself in the New Testament. Here we are two thousand years after Jesus walked the Earth and that portrait hasn't changed. He is unchanged in His Nature, Character, Person and Attributes.

God is Perfect

God must be Perfect to be God. God's Perfection can be used to prove God is immutable. If God is not perfect, He is no longer God. He must have always been perfect and He must always be perfect.

Let's say God can change. If He did, would He change for the better or for the worse? Let's assume that God has changed for the better. This would mean that He was not already perfect because He could become better. Could He make better decisions now? It would seem that all His decisions to this point may not have been Perfect.

Now let's switch sides and say He changed for the worse. He that was Perfect has become less than Perfect and therefore He can no longer be God. It makes sense that God must be Perfect and that any change implies either a departure from that perfection or a becoming perfect, meaning that He was not already perfect. Therefore, He must be perfect now and has always been perfect and will always be perfect and He can never change.

EXERCISE 1

Q1: There is no F______________ with God.

Q2: God can only be God if He is P__________.

Q3: If God changed for the B________, He must not have been Perfect.

God's Attributes Never Change

God's attributes are those aspects of Him that are essential to His Being. Without an attribute, God wouldn't be God. For instance, what are the necessary aspects of a table? It must be solid, flat, and have at least one leg. These are the attributes of a table. If a table is liquid or gas, it is no longer a table. If a table has no legs, it is no longer a table. Hence, if a table is missing one of its attributes, it ceases to be a table and becomes something else.

The same is true with God. God consists of different attributes. God is Holy, Faithful, Omniscient and so on. He would no longer be God if even one of these attributes of God were to change. If God's holiness were to be just a little unholy, He would not be God. If His faithfulness were to be just a little unfaithful, He would not be God. If any of His attributes changed just a little even for a short period of time, God would cease to be God. This is what it means that God is immutable. He never changes. If He ever did change, He would no longer be God. He doesn't choose to remain the same. He doesn't choose not to change. It is who He is. He is immutable. He cannot change.

God has always been the same. He was the same before Creation began and He will be the same forever. As discussed in Session 1, God is outside of Time and therefore incapable of changing. Since God is His attributes, and God never changes, we can deduce that His attributes never change. We can know that He will always be faithful, He will always be merciful, loving, gracious, all-powerful, all-knowing. His faithfulness is steadfast, His mercy is everlasting, His Love is eternal, His Grace is all-encompassing, His power is infinite, His knowledge is complete. These have always been true and will continue to be true. Whatever they were before is what they will always be.

God's Attribute of Faithfulness

I was attending a conference in San Diego several years ago. Lincoln Brewster and his band were playing the worship songs prior to Francis Chan coming up to speak. After the worship set was over but before Francis Chan took the stage, Lincoln Brewster seemingly spontaneously performed a moving rendition of "Great is Thy Faithfulness." The Holy Spirit filled the auditorium and every Christian in the place was moved to worship. When Francis Chan took to the microphone, he did so in tears and humility.

The Hymn that was at the center of this moment, "Great is Thy Faithfulness," sings of God's immutable attributes:

Great is Thy faithfulness, O God my Father;
There is no shadow of turning with Thee;
Thou changest not, Thy compassions, they fail not;
As Thou hast been, Thou forever will be.

Great is Thy Faithfulness! Great is Thy Faithfulness!
Morning by morning new mercies I see
All I have needed Thy Hands have provided
Great is Thy Faithfulness Lord unto me

How often have we sung that hymn and never realized it spoke to the immutability of God? See what the Hymn says: God's Great Faithfulness never changes because God never changes; His compassion and mercy never fails because God is the same yesterday and forever; God's provision for us continues daily and every need is satisfied; this will continue because the Faithfulness of God is to everlasting.

Yet, even though we may not have fully recognized the song's tribute to His immutability, didn't our hearts skip a beat? Didn't our spirits soar? We intrinsically recognize His immutable nature and it causes us to worship Him.

God's Attribute of Omniscience

Not only His faithfulness, but His knowledge also never changes. Some say that God does not know all things and that He is learning as He goes. They believe this because they read in the Bible that God has changed His mind. God said He would destroy Nineveh but then changed His mind. God made the Earth and Man upon it, but then repented of this and destroyed the Earth with the Flood. Their thinking is that God didn't know how things would turn out and therefore needed to change His mind after He gained new insight.

If this were true, then God would not know any better than you or I what is best for us. We would then be able to say God is ignorant about something. Think about it: If God is ignorant about anything, it would become possible for someone to know something that God did not know. We could be more knowledgeable about something than God is.

If God could gain knowledge, it would mean we could not trust God. He may or may not know what is best for the moment or for the future. Something might occur tomorrow, leading Him to break His promises. If God doesn't know everything about the future, can we have any assurance of salvation? How can we know that He is faithful when He might receive new information, forcing Him to change His mind? Our entire faith falls apart if God can gain knowledge.

Fortunately, God does know the beginning from the end! His knowledge is immutable. He knows everything that can be known, regardless of how far out in the future it may be. If God did not know something, then He would no longer be the only wise God (1 Timothy 1:17). But He is. God knows everything. There is nothing more for Him to know. Therefore, His knowledge never changes. He never receives new information that He has never known.

So why does the Bible say God changed His mind? God is simply telling us in His word that He is disappointed. He knew what would happen, but He is sorrowful about it. When He says He changed His mind or repented, He is teaching us about those things that are disheartening and disagreeable to Him. Yet, though He tells us His viewpoint "out loud," He doesn't change an iota of what He had planned to do from the beginning. He knew what men would do and what the outcome would be. He has never done something He didn't plan to do from the beginning.

God knows all things and He doesn't change His mind or His actions. He has all the knowledge He will ever need and has already determined how He will deal with each situation. His knowledge is complete. He will never have more or less knowledge than He has right now. This is also true with His faithfulness. It is true with all His attributes. His attributes are immutable.

EXERCISE 2

Q1: God's attributes are E_______________ to His Being.

Q2: If an attribute of God were to change, He would no long be G_____.

Q3: God's Faithfulness is Great. There is no S___________ of T__________ with Him.

Q4: God cannot G______ knowledge, for He already knows all that can be known.

CHAPTER EXERCISE

Think about a time when you had to make a choice. Why did you do it? Imagine you can go back in Time with the knowledge you now have. Would you have acted differently? How might that have changed your life? Imagine you are now living that new life. Go back to the beginning of this exercise and choose a different situation to change. Repeat the exercise. Do you see how God can do this for every situation? What does that tell you about God?

Session 3 – The Immutable Will of God

Elijah was a prophet of God. Around 850 BC, he found Elisha holding a yoke as he guided the oxen plowing the fields. That yoke might have been the most important piece of farming equipment he owned. Elijah took off his mantel and placed it on him as a sign that Elisha was to take on his role as the Prophet of God. Elisha then prepared a fire for a sacrifice using his yoke for fuel, which had been the tools of his livelihood just moments ago. Elisha was no longer a field-plowing farmer.

About 880 years later, Jesus taught us about His yoke. Using the tools of the commonplace farmer, Jesus instructed us that we can let go of the control we have over our lives and allow Jesus to take the reins. He tells us His yoke is easy should we decide to place it upon our shoulders.

As we move forward in history into the 1800's, we find American farmers continued to use oxen and yokes to cultivate the fields. Midway through that century, the steam engine is first used to drive a tractor that would do the tilling. In the 170 years since then, the tractor has gotten bigger and better and now plows most of the farms in the US. What might have taken Elisha days to plow now can take a farmer a few hours. Technology has certainly changed the way we work.

However, even with the internet, mobile phones and smart watches, we continue to look for easier ways to accomplish our work. Technology continues to have a major impact in the way we do things. Although oxen and yokes haven't quite gone the way of the passenger pigeon, most farmers are using newer technologies to produce their crops.

Technologies and civilizations have become unrecognizable to someone like Elisha. Yet, the human heart remains unchanged. Since the Fall of Adam, man has continued to kill, oppress and steal in order to attain the desires of their heart.

> *The heart is more deceitful than all else and is desperately sick; Who can understand it? – Jeremiah 17:9*
>
> *For out of the heart come evil thoughts, murders, adulteries, fornications, thefts, false witness, slanders. – Matthew 15:19*

Even so, we have a craving for a new heart:

> *Create in me a clean heart, O God, And renew a steadfast spirit within me. – Psalm 51:10*

We despise the one we have, knowing the evil that is in it, and we long for a change in our hearts. There seems to be nothing we can do to resolve this.

If that all rings true to you, then praise God! He has promised to give us that new heart.

> *And I will give them one heart, and put a new spirit within them. And I will take the heart of stone out of their flesh and give them a heart of flesh, – Ezekiel 11:19*
>
> *Moreover, I will give you a new heart and put a new spirit within you; and I will remove the heart of stone from your flesh and give you a heart of flesh. – Ezekiel 36:26*

Therefore if anyone is in Christ, he is a new creature; the old things passed away; behold, new things have come. – 2 Corinthians 5:17

Hundreds of years before Jesus was resurrected from the dead, God had promised that He would provide a way for us to receive new hearts. Then after Jesus rose from the dead, we learned we can receive these new hearts by trusting our lives to Jesus. When we are in Christ, we become new creatures and part of this newness is a new heart. We no longer need to worry about our wicked hearts because God has removed that heart of stone and replaced it with a heart of flesh.

But how can I know that I have this new heart? In most cases, you can feel it internally. You think differently than you used to. Things that were good or acceptable are now evil and sinful. You are amazed that you used to think the same way that the world does. In other cases, your family, friends and coworkers will witness to you the change they see. You no longer come across as angry, impatient, arrogant or intolerant and now seem to be gentle, loving and at peace. In any case, we can know we have this new heart because God has promised it in His word to those who truly trust in Him and His Promises never change. They are immutable.

The Immutability of His Word

Forever, O Lord,
Your word is settled in heaven. – Psalm 119:89

That God's word never changes has important ramifications.

If God's word changed, there would be "prophets" popping up all over and telling us new revelations about God and Jesus. There would be many like Charles Taze Russell, who became just such a "prophet" and today we have the Jehovah's Witnesses.

If God's word changed, reading the Bible would become problematic. The Bible has many truths contained within it. However, these truths could change at the word of a teacher who has had an utterance from God. The old "truth" is gone; a new one has taken its place.

If God's word changed, we could not trust any of the promises God has given us. Will all my needs be satisfied if I seek first the kingdom of God and His righteousness? Has the Holy Spirit been sent to be my Advocate? Am I a new creation when I believe? Are we going to Heaven by His Grace through faith in Jesus? Do I have a new heart? Every one of these promises would only be good until someone prophesied otherwise.

If God's word changed, there would be no way for us to know God. His word is our definitive source for knowing Him. Otherwise, we would have to depend on revelations and dreams to determine who and what God is. God would have to show Himself over and over so that each generation might know Him again.

Fortunately, these things are not issues for us. God's word does not change. God Himself is immutable and outside of Time. His thoughts and His words are immutable and outside of Time. Therefore, we can cast aside any prophet giving a new revelation, any teacher changing a commandment or anyone amending a promise of God. We can trust His word. We can know His promises never change.

We can know God Himself because He has revealed Himself in His word and it never changes. God has given us an understanding of Who He is. We would never know about the Creator, the Savior or the Advocate if it weren't for the word of God. Since His word never changes, we can know these things, deepening our knowledge and understanding of Him.

EXERCISE 1

Q1: God's W________ never changes.

Q2: We can believe that the Bible is T________.

Q3: Since the Bible is true, we can K________ God.

Q4: God R__________________ Himself in the Bible.

A Real World Application

Today, we see a battle going on for the word of God. Many Christians are adamant that the Bible must be taken as it is written. This is an important battle for us. If the word of God is allowed to change, then God loses. The God of the Bible no longer exists and some other, false, god takes His place.

This is why secularists try so hard to remove God from Creation. If the Earth, the Universe and Life developed over millions of years, then the Bible cannot be trusted to be truthful regarding anything, including the Person of God. If God did not create everything in six days and rest on the seventh, then He probably also didn't destroy the Earth by a great flood, disperse the people at the Tower of Babel, destroy Sodom and Gomorrah, part the Red Sea or send His Son to be the sacrifice for sin.

Unfortunately, this is exactly what has happened. Let's analyze each example above based on the reality that most Christians have accepted the secular concept of a billions-of-years-old universe. Following is the thinking that has been birthed from unbelief in a literal understanding of God's Creation in six days:

- God did not create everything in six days. The Universe was created over billions of years.
- God did not destroy the world by a flood; that is just a myth. However, the dinosaurs were destroyed by a massive meteor shower millions of years ago.

- The Tower of Babel is a myth. The people of the Earth have spoken many languages for tens of thousands of years. Languages came about because different tribes in distant places gradually learned to communicate in new ways over many years.
- The sin of Sodom and Gomorrah was that they were uncharitable and abusive to strangers. It could not have been that they were performing acts of homosexuality because: not *all* the men could have been homosexual; Lot wouldn't have offered his daughters if he knew they were all gay; and there wouldn't have been any children. Certainly, a loving God would never have killed all the women and children of Sodom because of a few gay men.
- God did not part the Red Sea. The Israelites crossed the Reed Sea, which is a reedy lake much nearer to the land of Goshen. Since reeds can only grow in fresh water, the Israelites could not have crossed the Red Sea. However, Moses knew the tides based on the moon. When the tides were low and the wind was strong, the Reed Sea bottom would dry, allowing people to walk through without danger.

These are all beliefs inside and outside the Church. It should not surprise us. Once natural reasons are given for the things God has done, it is only a matter of time before everything has a natural explanation and God has done nothing. How long before Jesus is simply a good man who was misunderstood?

The point of this section was to show the slippery slope upon which Bible believers walk when they allow a secular belief system to determine what is true. Christians must adhere to the Bible for their truth. Many Christians insist that we cannot ignore science to keep our blind faith. I will simply say that the immutability of the Bible was also believed by the greatest scientists in History, including: Galileo, Copernicus, Newton, Kepler, Pascal, Boyle and Babbage. Babbage wrote, "*There exists no fatal collision between the words of Scripture and the facts of nature.*" The word of God doesn't need to change to fit secular science. In fact, the word of God never changes.

The Promises of God Remain

> *"God is not a man, that He should lie,*
> *Nor a son of man, that He should repent;*
> *Has He said, and will He not do it?*
> *Or has He spoken, and will He not make it good? – Num 23:19*

Many years ago, I worked in Manhattan. For me, the Long Island Railroad was the best way to commute. The advantage of travelling by train is that you can work or read while you go back and forth. My afternoon rush hour routine was to take the train to Stony Brook, get in my car and drive fifteen minutes to Port Jefferson to pick up the kids at daycare since Jackie was working.

Often, if I was too tired to work or read, I would drift off to sleep. I became adept at waking before reaching the train station. On one particular day, I must have been exhausted because when I awoke, I had missed my stop. Immediately, my thoughts went to the children. Without a car, I had to get to the nursery before they closed. Thankfully, the train stop in Port Jeff was only a couple of miles from where the children were. I was able to run there, get the kids and call Jackie for a ride.

As I ran, I was worried, upset and nervous. I broke so many promises that day: a promise to my wife that I would be reliable, a promise to my children that I would be there, a promise to the nursery that I would be timely, a promise to myself that I would be a good father. I made another promise during that run: I would never fall asleep on the train again.

Our problem is that we human beings make many promises that we are unable to keep. It's not that we make the promises with the intention of breaking them. Things come up. Situations change. Accidents occur. When someone makes a promise to us, we expect them to keep it. However, we are usually gracious to them when they break that promise because we know that these things happen and that frequently, we are on the offending side. As often as people break promises to us, we break them to others.

Isn't it good to know that God is not like us? When God makes a promise, we can be confident He will keep His promise. In Numbers, we read, "Has He said and will He not do it? Or has He spoken and will He not make it good?" If God has promised us something, we do not need to worry that some circumstance will cause Him to break that promise.

> *If I thought that the notes of the bank of England could not be cashed next week, I should decline to take them; and if I thought that God's promises would never be fulfilled—if I thought that God would see it right to alter some word in his promises—farewell Scriptures! – Charles Spurgeon*[1]

Since God's knowledge is complete and He knows everything that will happen, we can be confident that He will do what He promised. Since God is all-powerful, we can know that His arms are not too short and He will complete what He started. When we break our promises, it is because we did not know something or did not have the ability to fulfill it. Our lack of foreknowledge means unexpected situations will arise. Our lack of power means we will not be able to impose our will upon many circumstances. This is why we break our promises. God does not have these issues.

This is eerily comforting. While we know how unfaithful we can be in keeping our promises, we can be fully secure knowing that God is unfailingly faithful in keeping His. So, we can know we are saved because He has told us we are when we trust in Jesus. We can know we will be in Heaven because Jesus has promised He is preparing a place for us there. We can know we have God's Holy Spirit because Jesus promised to send Him to us. We can know we are forgiven, that God will provide for us, and that we will be resurrected to be with Him forever. These are promises given to us by God and His promises are immutable. When God makes a plan, He will not veer off course.

> *"Remember the former things long past,*
> *For I am God, and there is no other;*
> *I am God, and there is no one like Me,*
> *Declaring the end from the beginning,*
> *And from ancient times things which have not been done,*
> *Saying, 'My purpose will be established,*
> *And I will accomplish all My good pleasure';*
> *Calling a bird of prey from the east,*

---

1 "The Immutability of God" – Sermon by Charles Spurgeon – 1855

The man of My purpose from a far country.
Truly I have spoken; truly I will bring it to pass.

I have planned it, surely I will do it. – Isaiah 46:9-11

EXERCISE 2

Q1: We can be C________________ that God will do what He promised.

Q2: God's K________________ is complete. Nothing can happen to make Him break His promise.

Q3: God is A_____-P______________. He will complete what He started.

Q4: When God makes a plan, nothing can cause Him to V_____ off course.

CHAPTER EXERCISE

We have all been affected by the thinking of our time and culture. Yet it is our Christian duty to remain firm by thinking and living Biblically. Where have you been influenced by the thinking of the world? Some areas to start: were the stars created before the Earth; how many races of humans are there; does everything need to have a natural explanation; was God morally wrong to destroy Sodom? In what other areas might secular society be influencing you? What changes do you need to make based on this?

Session 4 – The Immutability of Jesus

Jesus the God

In the beginning was the Word, and the Word was with God, and the Word was God. He was with God in the beginning. Through him all things were made; without him nothing was made that has been made. – John 1:1-3

The Bible is clear that Jesus is God. He is the Son of God, the Second Person of the Trinity. He was in the beginning and therefore He is eternal. He created all things and therefore He is omnipotent. Throughout the Gospels, we hear Jesus telling people that He is God. It is because of this, the people try to stone him and the religious leaders have him crucified.

Many people claim Jesus never actually said He was God. They are mistaken. Those who say this are English speakers who do not understand the language of Jesus' day. Jesus was crystal clear that He was God when He said, "My Father is always at His work to this very day, and I too am working." As people living in the 21st century, we do not see how that statement tells us that Jesus is God. However, it does. We can know that by the reaction of the people who heard it.

So, because Jesus was doing these things on the Sabbath, the Jewish leaders began to persecute him. In his defense Jesus said to them, "My Father is always at his work to this very day, and I too am working." For this reason they tried all the more to kill him; not only was he breaking the Sabbath, but he was even calling God his own Father, making himself equal with God. – John 5:16-18

The religious leaders desperately wanted to end Jesus' life because they saw Him as someone who was bringing people down a wrong path. Why did they think this? Because they did not believe Jesus was God and yet Jesus kept calling Himself God. Though they are not able to convict Him for doing anything wrong (since Jesus was sinless, for He was holy as God is holy), they are able to convict Him for calling Himself God:

The high priest said to him, "I charge you under oath by the living God: Tell us if you are the Messiah, the Son of God."
"You have said so," Jesus replied. "But I say to all of you: From now on you will see the Son of Man sitting at the right hand of the Mighty One and coming on the clouds of heaven."
Then the high priest tore his clothes and said, "He has spoken blasphemy! Why do we need any more witnesses? Look, now you have heard the blasphemy. What do you think?"

" He is worthy of death," they answered.

– Matthew 26:63-66

In English, we would expect Jesus to have said the words, "I am God." However, He does not say those exact words but instead admits to being the Son of God and the Son of Man. He also says that He will sit at the right hand of God and come on the clouds of heaven. Though we do not hear, "I am God," it is because we are from a different time and place. The religious leaders heard it and it was the evidence they needed to have Him put to death.

The beginning of the Gospel of Mark gives us unquestioned evidence that Mark understood Jesus to be God.

> *The beginning of the good news about Jesus the Messiah, the Son of God, as it is written in Isaiah the prophet:*
> *"I will send my messenger ahead of you,*
> *who will prepare your way"—*
> *"a voice of one calling in the wilderness,*
> *'Prepare the way for the Lord,*
> *make straight paths for him.'" – Mark 1:1-3*

Our normal reading of this passage doesn't tell us much. In fact, it seems to introduce us to John the Baptist rather than Jesus. However, the early readers of this Gospel would have heard clearly that Jesus was God. First, Mark starts with the phrase, "Jesus the Messiah, the Son of God." We've already seen how the phrase, "Son of God" equated Jesus with God.

Mark doesn't stop there. He goes on to quote the prophets Malachi and Isaiah.

> *"Behold, I am going to send My messenger, and he will clear the way before Me. And the Lord, whom you seek, will suddenly come to His temple; and the messenger of the covenant, in whom you delight, behold, He is coming," says the Lord of hosts. – Malachi 3:1*

> *A voice is calling,*
> *"Clear the way for the Lord in the wilderness;*
> *Make smooth in the desert a highway for our God. – Isaiah 40:3*

Notice who the subject is in both of these prophesies. It is God. In Malachi, God says *He* is sending *His* messenger who will clear the way before *Him*. They are seeking *God*. *God* is coming. In Isaiah, the voice that is calling is clearing *God's* way, leveling *God's* path. These verses are about God and Mark has chosen these verses for the specific reason that he is equating Jesus to God. He is showing that God has come, just as He prophesied He would through the Old Testament prophets. God has come as Jesus.

EXERCISE 1

Q1: The Gospels of M_______ and J_______ both begin with the clear statement that Jesus is God.

Q2: Those who say Jesus never said he was God are M____________.

Q3: The religious leaders tried to kill Jesus because he made himself E_______ to God.

Q4: The Sanhedrin found Jesus guilty of B_______________ and had him crucified because he said he was the Son of God and the Son of Man.

Jesus the Man

While the Gospels of Mark and John begin with the Deity of Jesus, the Gospels of Matthew and Luke begin with his humanity. Both Matthew and Luke give us the Nativity accounts we have grown so accustomed to hearing every Christmas. Though they give us different aspects and views of the birth of Jesus, they make one undeniable point: Jesus was born as a Man.

Luke continues his Gospel of Jesus in the Book of Acts. In Acts, we read about Peter and Paul both calling Jesus a Man:

> *"Men of Israel, listen to these words: Jesus the Nazarene, a man attested to you by God with miracles and wonders and signs which God performed through Him in your midst, just as you yourselves know—this Man, delivered over by the predetermined plan and foreknowledge of God, you nailed to a cross by the hands of godless men and put Him to death. – Peter in Acts 2:22-23*
>
> *Therefore having overlooked the times of ignorance, God is now declaring to men that all people everywhere should repent, because He has fixed a day in which He will judge the world in righteousness through a Man whom He has appointed, having furnished proof to all men by raising Him from the dead." – Paul in Acts 17:30-31*

Jesus the God-Man

When we read the Bible as a whole, we come to recognize that Jesus is both. He is God. He is Man. He is not partially God and partially Man. He is as much God as the Father and the Spirit. He is as much Man as you and I. Philippians 2:5-11 explains:

> *Have this attitude in yourselves which was also in Christ Jesus, who, although He existed in the form of God, did not regard equality with God a thing to be grasped, but emptied Himself, taking the form of a bond-servant, and being made in the likeness of men. Being found in appearance as a man, He humbled Himself by becoming obedient to the point of death, even death on a cross. For this reason also, God highly exalted Him, and bestowed on Him the name which is above every name, so that at the name of Jesus every knee will bow, of those who are in heaven and on earth and under the earth, and that every tongue will confess that Jesus Christ is Lord, to the glory of God the Father.*

Notice that Christ Jesus "existed" in the form of God. When Paul says this, he is telling us that Jesus has always existed. He is eternal. The term "form of God" tells us that Jesus had the God-substance, the essence, which makes him the same as God. Plants are made of stuff that makes them plants. Plant cells, chloroplasts and photosynthesis are all part of what makes a plant. Animals are made of stuff that makes them animals. Eating, moving, having organs and muscles are all part of what makes an animal. As we are learning in this study, God is made up of stuff that makes Him God. Being Spirit, Holy, Eternal and Infinite are all part of what makes God.

Therefore, Jesus, though he was eternal and was in the form of God, took on the form of Man. He now also had the substance of Man. He did not replace His form of God with the form of Man. He added it on. Being Man, He who was spirit was now physical. He who was eternal now had a beginning and an end. Jesus was no longer simply God. He was now God-Man.

When Jesus became Man, He did not stop being God. God cannot stop being God. Many believe that Jesus left His God-substance in Heaven because they have misunderstood what it means that He emptied Himself to become Man. If this were to be true, then God has changed and is no longer the same God as He was before.

God has always been and will always be Triune. It is the heresy of the Jehovah's Witnesses and the Arians before them to think that Jesus was not God. These heretics do not believe Jesus can be God because they know that God cannot change and they cannot understand how God became Man. Their response to this is to reject the deity of Jesus.

However, to reject Christ's deity means we need to reinterpret much of scripture, for the Bible, from start to finish, gives us a Christ who is God Himself. Therefore, the Jehovah's Witnesses have reinterpreted Jesus to be the Archangel Michael. Any non-Jehovah's Witness reading the Bible will find this interpretation to be incredible. No normal reading of the Scriptures allows for this. This is what happens when we confuse the dual natures of Jesus.

How then are we to understand that Jesus was God, that God has never changed and yet Jesus became Man? Our difficulty comes from misunderstanding the Person of Jesus. He is two natures in one Person. The two natures are the nature of Deity and the nature of Man. Our confusion comes when we think of this as a mixture when it should be better understood as a binding.

As an example, when we mix sugar and water, the two become one. We now have sweet water. We cannot separate these without destroying the whole. This is how we typically think about the person of Christ. We recognize the two natures in one person and assume they are mixed together. Just as sugar and water become "sugarwater," we have mixed the natures of Jesus to make him "godman."

However, there is a better way. When we mix oil and vinegar, no matter how hard we shake, the two substances never dissolve into each other and always will separate. Though they become dressing, they are always separate. Binding the two ingredients together has created one new thing: dressing. This is how it is with the person of Christ. His two natures never mix. Deity never becomes Humanity and Humanity never becomes Deity. These two natures remain separate and pure even as they exist within the One Person of Jesus.

Therefore, it is right to say the Man Jesus has changed. He did not exist, but now he does. However, the God Jesus is the same as He has always been. He is the same yesterday, today and forever (Hebrews 13:8). When Jesus took on the form of man, he never let go of the form of God. Jesus did not stop being God when He emptied Himself (Phil 2:7). He did not remove any part of Himself that would cause Him to cease being God. When the scriptures speak of His emptying Himself, it is speaking of His humility. In this humility, he gave up the *privileges* of being God. Yet, He never ceased to be the same God He was before He became Man. Like the prince who swaps his identity with the pauper and temporarily lives the hard life of a working class boy, nevertheless he remains the prince and will soon return to his throne.

If Jesus gave up just one aspect of being God, we could no longer call him God. He would not be fully God and fully Man. He would then have become an extraordinary man, but he would not be God. If for one second, God did not have every attribute of God, He would no longer be God. If Jesus did not have every attribute of God, He would no longer be God.

If Jesus was not God, his death on the cross was useless. While it is required that a Man must pay for the sins that have been committed by men, no man can ever pay enough. Only an infinite God can pay the price for all the sins that have been committed. Therefore, if Jesus was not the Infinite God, we would not have a sufficient sacrifice. God could not accept the sacrifice of Jesus any more than He could accept my death for the forgiveness of all men, even if I never sinned.

However, there is a way for us to know that Jesus' sacrifice was acceptable to God. The evidence is the Resurrection of Jesus. If Jesus never rose again, his rotted corpse would be the evidence that proved he was just a man. Since He did resurrect, then it must follow that the One who died on the cross was God for He is the only One who can pay the price of all our sins. Jesus became Man because the sins of Man can only be paid for by another Man. However, He must have been God because only God can pay that price.

Jesus is the God-Man, two natures, one person, whose natures never mix. As a Man, Jesus certainly changed. As God, He never changed. Everything that makes God Deity was found in Jesus. Jesus chose to empty Himself. He never gave up the things that made Him God. He humbly gave up the use of those things. Jesus continued to be God, even as he became Man. As God, He has never changed. He is the same yesterday, today and forever. As God, Jesus is immutable.

EXERCISE 2

Q1: Jesus E____________ in the F______ of God

Q2: Although Jesus E___________ Himself and became Man, He remained God.

Q3: His natures of God and Man never M________ together.

Q4: The evidence that Jesus was both God and Man is found in his R__________________.

"What peace it brings to the Christian's heart to realize that our Heavenly Father never differs from Himself... Today, this moment, He feels toward His creatures, toward babies, toward the sick, the fallen, the sinful, exactly as He did when He sent His only-begotten Son into the world to die for mankind." – A.W. Tozer[2]

CHAPTER EXERCISE

In the quote by Tozer, he equates peace with God's immutability. Meditate for a few minutes on his words, "our Heavenly Father never differs from Himself."

- *What emotions did you experience? Did you encounter the peace Tozer mentions? Any other feelings come over you? Write this down in the space below.*

Now meditate for a few minutes on the second part of Tozer's quote.

- *What emotions did you experience this time? Write this down in the space below.*

Jesus Christ is the same yesterday and today and forever. – Hebrews 13:8

Meditate on this verse from the Book of Hebrews.

- *One more time, what emotions did you experience? Write them down below.*

---

[2] Knowledge of the Holy by A.W. Tozer pg 57; Harper and Row 1975

Session 5 – Takeaways

A Time for Meditation

As we complete our study of the immutability of God, we will spend some time meditating on the truths we have learned. Read each statement below and spend 30-seconds meditating on each. Fully reflect on each statement before going on to the next.

- God doesn't choose to remain the same; He cannot change.
- God cannot change because He is outside of Time.
- That God calls Himself "I AM" is appropriate.
- God never changes in His Person: His attributes, His character, His nature, His being – Who He Is.
- God never changes in His Will: His purposes, His promises, His word – What He Does.
- God can only be God if He has always been Perfect; no better, no worse, ever.
- God cannot gain knowledge for then He would not have been all-knowing.
- God's word never changes.
- Since God reveals Himself in His word, we can know God today.
- God is able to do what He said because He is Omnipotent and His power cannot be greater.
- God never has to change His mind since He has perfect knowledge of all future things.
- Jesus is fully God and fully Man and these two natures never mix in His Person.
- Since Jesus is God, He never changes in His Godly nature; only Jesus' Human nature changes.

The Importance of God's Immutability

We've just spent four sessions on the Immutability of God. Why is this significant?

We have confidence regarding the Person of God. Since God is immutable, we know who He is. Since He never changes, He is the same today as He was when He first revealed Himself to men. When Adam and Eve first saw God, they spoke to the same God we speak to today. We don't have to worry that God's heart has shifted since He first gave Moses His commands. We don't have to be concerned that God has changed. We can be sure of whom God is.

We can depend on His Promises. Since God is immutable, we know that His will is the same as when He gave His promises to His prophets and His apostles. We can hold tight to them. The Bible is true. God will care for us. Even if we are living through difficult times, He will sustain us. He has a plan for His Church that is better than we can imagine and though we may not experience this here, we will in Heaven. We know this because He has promised He will work all things for our good.

We can be sure of the future. Since God is immutable, we know Jesus is preparing a place for us where He is. He will return to take us to be where He is. We will live in a new Earth with a new Heaven and God will live with us to be our light. God has promised us that our sins have been forgiven when we received Jesus, that we have become His adopted children and that He will give us eternal life. All these things are true for us as they were for those 2,000-years ago. They will continue to be true for as long as sinful man walks on the Earth.

We can be certain of God's attributes. Since God is immutable, His attributes never change. Therefore, He is always faithful. We can know that all He has said is still true and that He will keep His promises. He is always all-powerful. He is able to do whatever is needed to fulfill those promises. He is always all-knowing. He knows everything that has happened, is happening and will happen and nothing will come to pass that will surprise Him. There is nothing more for Him to know and He cannot grow in knowledge because He knows all things. He is always love. There is nothing that can occur to change His love for us or remove it from us.

We can be unrestrained in our worship. Since God is immutable, we worship Him uninhibited by any doubt. We worship Him for who He is because He has not changed. We will worship Him in Heaven because He is the same God then and there as He is here and now. We worship Him together with the angels since we are worshipping the same God they have known since they were first created. Since He hasn't changed an iota, we can worship Him with the saints of old: Adam, Noah, Abraham, Joseph; Moses, Joshua, David, Daniel; Peter, John, James and Paul. We all worship the same God.

We can be assured of our salvation. Since God is immutable in His person and His will, we know He desires for us not to perish. Instead, He offers us eternal life through His Son. Nothing can ever happen to change this. Jesus has died. God has roared by the Resurrection of Christ, "His death is sufficient for the forgiveness of sins!" Nothing anyone can do will alter this. He has done it. He has said it. It is finished. Salvation is now available to any who would receive Jesus. Since God never changes, we are secure in this knowledge forever.

We can have Hope. Since God is immutable, we are guaranteed those promises for us regarding our future. He said we will suffer trouble in this world. Yet our hope is not in this world but in eternity. Since God has also promised that He is preparing a place for His children where He lives, we can know we will live with God in His presence forever. No matter what happens in this world, we have hope. The culture we live in might become dire and vile. The world around us might change. God does not. He is our rock and our salvation even as everything else is sinking sand.

CHAPTER 3

Omniscience

We believe that God is Omniscient. To say God is Omniscient is to mean He knows all things. All humans assume God is Omniscient, whether they believe in God or not. Silent prayer is based on His Omniscience. We know God sees what is in our hearts and knows what we think. We depend on His Omniscience when we do good works in secret. We expect to be rewarded for these good works in the next life and we count on His Omniscience to know accurately everything we have done that has gone unnoticed by the world.

If God were not Omniscient, He might not know about some sins we may have committed. We would not need to fear any future punishment or consequences. We would get away with our sinful actions. Even better, we would enter into Heaven as well. If God were not Omniscient, He would not know our hearts. Therefore, He would not be able to judge our hearts nor our hidden, sinful actions since He has not seen them.

Yet, we know He does see. He knows everything we are doing. More importantly, He knows everything we are thinking and everything that is in our hearts. He is Omniscient and in the most fundamental ways, we know and understand this.

Our way of visualizing His Omniscience is by thinking of Him watching over us. Although God is Spirit, we think of Him with eyes that can see both our physical activities as well as the spiritual and emotional things within us.

Since ancient times, all religions have recognized that God is Omniscient. Many religions believe in more than one god. In those religions, at least one of their gods has omniscience. Often, it is one of their greatest gods. Remembering that God commanded His people never to make an image of Him, Jews and Christians don't have icons or statues of God. However, most every other religion in history did make idols to worship and most of them use the eye as a symbol of their god's omniscience.

- In Hinduism, one of the three greatest gods they worship is named Shiva. You will recognize the images of Shiva by his third eye. This eye represents his omniscience.
- In Buddhism, there is the Eyes of Buddha. Again, there is a third eye, more of a circle between the usual two eyes, which represent wisdom. In their stupas, which are monuments commemorating a sacred place or event, the Eyes of Buddha represent the all-seeing ability of the Buddha.

- In ancient Egyptian mythology, we find the Eye of Horus. Horus was a sky god, later becoming the sun god. With his perspective in the sky, he could see all things, which is why the Eye of Horus is also known as the all-seeing eye.
- Archeology has found the eye symbol in Aztec and Native American Indian artifacts.

Every religion recognizes the Omniscience of God. Anyone who believes God exists must recognize His Omniscience. Otherwise, their sacrifices, prayers, temple worships and oaths would be worthless. If God is not Omniscient, these have been given to a blind God who can neither reward nor punish things of which He does not know. Yet, everyone knows that God does see.

The Fathers of America saw fit to have the all-seeing eye as part of the Great Seal of the United States. You can find this on the back of a one-dollar bill. This eye depicted God's omniscience. It is enclosed in a triangle, representing the Triune God, and surrounded by rays of light, depicting the Light and the Glory of God. The idea was that God was watching over the nation, symbolized by the thirteen levels of the pyramid.

The Bible often describes God's Omniscience by speaking of His seeing and watching. In 2 Chronicles 16:9, we read,

> *"For the eyes of the LORD move to and fro throughout the earth that He may strongly support those whose heart is completely His."*

This verse exemplifies God's omniscience. He can see throughout the earth. He can see into the heart. The idea of His eyes moving to and fro implies He is always watching. Hence, nothing gets past our God. There is nothing He does not know.

Whether the secular symbols of America or the symbols of religions throughout time, humans seem to intuitively know that someone greater than ourselves is watching over us. From ancient times to the present, we recognize that God knows all things.

Session 1 – Types of Knowledge

When we think of knowledge, we think of science. The word "science" means knowledge, though today we have narrowed that down more specifically to mean knowledge acquired by experimentation. When I was in school, my favorite part of Science classes was doing experiments. I attended one class for every other subject, but for Science, I attended two: one for lecture and one for lab. Those experiments took place in these lab classes.

These labs were hands-on classes that allowed us to experience how the Scientific Method works. The teacher would give us a hypothesis and we would do experiments to determine whether that hypothesis was correct. Once we came to a conclusion, we would have to repeat the experiment to see if the outcome occurred by chance or if it was something that could be expected every time. When a repeated experiment resulted in the same conclusion consistently, we could know that the hypothesis was right.

I remember one of our experiments was to drop two objects of different weights and sizes to see which would fall fastest. Most of us would drop the objects from about shoulder height. But that wasn't good enough for Billy. It didn't make sense that something larger and heavier was falling at the same speed as something smaller and lighter. He needed to get up on a table and drop things from above his head. When that wasn't enough, he went to the window of our second floor classroom and started dropping things out the window. Though Billy got in trouble for that experiment, we all learned about gravity.

Yet, there is more to knowledge than simply repeated experiments. There must be something behind these Scientific conclusions that enable them to be immutable. Why are they true yesterday, today and tomorrow? How can we depend on these conclusions to not change?

When the Jesuit China mission in the 16th and 17th centuries returned to Europe, they made known the achievements of the Ancient Chinese. According to Joseph Needham, these ancients had earthquake detectors, matches, the decimal system, cast iron, the propeller, and solid fuel rockets, among others. However, they never developed these into "modern science" because of their belief in Tao, which states that the nature of Nature is not static. They didn't recognize that God created the Universe with laws that He sustains (Colossians 1:17).

Yet, we know God created the Universe. As Creator of all things, He knows the details of everything He has created. Nothing exists that He doesn't know about.

Knowledge of Things that Exist

We live in a naturalistic culture. By this, I mean that the authorities are always forcing upon us the idea that reality consists of only those things that we can experience with our five senses. Therefore, everything is explained by the natural laws. If something happens that is unexplainable, "Time" becomes the all encompassing solution. In other words, everything that exists has an origin that can be explained by "science." If "science" doesn't have the explanation, then they simply haven't discovered the natural law behind it yet, but they will over time.

By "authorities," I mean those who control the information given to the masses. This includes the government, the education system, the media and so on – those who supposedly have the knowledge. Interestingly, at this time in history, although these "authorities" continue to push this naturalistic worldview, indoctrinating our children with evolution, implementing immoral social agendas and propagating secular propaganda, the majority of the masses still believe in the supernatural, specifically in God.

This is both understandable and heartening. It is understandable because the Bible teaches us that we are spiritual and therefore, more than simply natural beings. It is heartening because it means that even when Satan, the god of this world, has taken over the "authorities" in this age, God still has the hearts and minds of the people. The people of God know that there is more to reality than meets the eye. We know there is both that which we can see and that which we cannot. Paul tells us about this reality:

> *For by Him all things were created, both in the heavens and on earth, visible and invisible, whether thrones or dominions or rulers or authorities—all things have been created through Him and for Him.*
> *– Colossians 1:16*

The Bible teaches that God created all things. Of course, Paul could have stopped writing there, recognizing that "all things" means everything. But our God is not a God who is hasty to leave us without details. So He gives us a definition of "all things" and explains that it means:

Things in the heavens

Things on the earth

Things visible

Things invisible

These four things make up everything that exists. When Paul writes "in the heavens," he does not mean Heaven, as in the place where God's throne is, Jesus sitting at His right hand and the angels worshipping. Elsewhere in scripture, this would be called the "third heaven" (2 Corinthians 12:2). Here, Paul is writing about the celestial heaven: the sun, the moon and the stars.

We live in a day when cities own the landscape. Even those of us who live in suburbs are affected by the lights of the nearby cities. According to the US Census Bureau, 81-percent of America lives in urban areas. So when the Bible speaks of the glories of the heavens, we don't really understand its meaning. We look up in the night sky and are barely impressed with the moon and the stars we see. However, get far away from the large cities and it is impossible not to be awed by the heavens.

When we get a chance to see the night sky as our ancestors did, we can understand their awe of God. The stars in the heavens are innumerable. Yet, God knows the number of the stars and He knows their name (Psalm 147:4). God knows this because He created them. This is true not only of the stars but of the planets that encircle them and their moons. He knows every black hole, nebula, solar system, galaxy, asteroid, comet or super-nova. He created all the things in the heavens. That we are told, "He calls them by name," means that He is intimately knowledgeable about them. There is nothing in the heavens that He doesn't know about.

Coming down to Earth, nothing changes. There is nothing on this planet that God does not know about. As He has created all things in the heavens, He has also created all things on the Earth. He thoroughly knows every person, animal, bird or fish that lives or has lived. He knows each tree, plant and insect that exists. He knows the mountains, valleys, oceans and ponds. Not a grain of sand, wheat or salt exists that He doesn't know about. All things on Earth have been created by Him and He knows every single one of them.

We recognize that everything we've mentioned is material. We can see or sense each one. God has created all things visible. If that was the end of it, we would bow down and honor the God who has made the visible universe. However, it is not the end. We already discussed that we know there is more to reality that just the physical. There is the supernatural, that which we cannot sense, which is invisible.

God knows everything about the invisible. He created all the invisible things. The Heavenly realm (this time speaking of the Heaven where God is and Jesus is at His right hand) was created by Him. There is nothing in Heaven that He does not know about. Jesus has gone there to prepare a place for us and will return to take us there (John 14:2-3). Since He is the one preparing it for us, certainly He knows all about it.

He knows what the Heavenly Realm consists of, how it is and how it will be. He knows what is in it. He knows the angels that worship there. He knows the brethren who currently reside there, those who have passed away and wait anxiously for the resurrection of the dead. Outside of Heaven, there is no aspect of the spiritual realm that God does not know about. The whereabouts of each demon and of Satan is known by God.

And so, God knows all things that exist.

EXERCISE 1

Q1: The world believes only in the N________ but we know the S________________ is real as well.

Q2: The four aspects that make up reality are the things in H__________, on E________, and the V_________ as well as the I_____________.

Q3: That God knows everything's name means that He knows them I_____________.

Tonight, look up at the night sky, regardless of where you are, take the time to experience the awesomeness of God.

Knowledge of the Possible

God is not only knowledgeable of the things that exist, but He also knows about all nonexistent things. Many possible creatures have not been created. Many possible situations have not occurred. God knows about every one of them.

That may seem like a lot to know! It is for finite humans such as we are, but for God, it is what He is. We can understand God's knowledge of all things that exists. However, when it comes to His knowledge of all things that are possible and yet have never or will never exist, our minds cannot comprehend this. Isn't our God awesome?! It is comforting to know that we have a God who is beyond our comprehension. Personally, I wouldn't want to worship a god whom I could fully understand. I recognize that God is too great for me ever to fully wrap my mind around.

Since we are discussing things that are possible but never existed, it is foolishness to think we can know all aspects of these possible realities. We are entering into a place of philosophy rather than concrete truths. Yet it is important for us to take this trip if we are to grasp a little of the extent of God's Omniscience. We can never enter into the mind of God to understand the things of God. Only His Spirit can do this (1 Corinthians 2:11). Even so, we will attempt to make some logical deductions based on our current knowledge of God. While we cannot know the extent of all possible realities, for the sake of discussion, I will break them down into two categories: things and actions.

Regarding the things that don't exist, God knows each one. Recognizing that God knows what is best, He has created all things towards that end. God could have created things differently, but He knew that making humans with three arms would not be best. He could have made an animal that followed humans around and did everything they were asked, but God knew that would not be best. He could have created a creature that had seven eyes and could hear all frequencies of the sound spectrum but He knew that would not be best.

Regarding actions that have never occurred, God knows each one. He knows what didn't happen when you fell and almost hit your head. He knows what didn't happen when David first saw Bathsheba on the roof. He knows what didn't happen when America was deciding whether or not to break away from the British Empire. God knows each action that could have occurred but didn't.

Our logic tells us that if God knows what is best, then He will make that happen. If any of these nonexistent things would have made things better, He would have created them. If any of these nonexistent actions would have made things better, He would have enabled them. He has not because He knows where these would lead and that they would not lead to a better place but to a worse one. Therefore, in His Omniscience, He has seen them, analyzed their impact and determined that they would be worse for eternity than had He allowed them to exist.

If God does not know about every possible thing or action, then there is a chance that something could have made things better. This would mean that God did not know this and is therefore not Omniscient. If there was something God could have allowed to exist that would have made eternity better or brought Himself more glory and didn't, it means that He did not have enough knowledge to make the proper decisions regarding Eternity and His Glory. Instead of saying God is Omniscient, we would have to say that He is the most knowledgeable of all that exists. That is very different from Omniscient and it lowers Him from God to simply superior.

If God is to be Omniscient, He must know about all possible things, even if they never existed or never will exist.

EXERCISE 2

Q1: God knows about things that are N______________as well as things that exist.

Q2: T________ and A________ are two categories of the Possible of which we can know God has complete knowledge.

Q3: God would have created something that currently doesn't exist if He knew that it would make things for the B_______ in eternity or brought Him more G________.

Q4: For God to be O______________, He must know everything that is P________.

CHAPTER EXERCISE

> He determines the number of the stars
> and calls them each by name.
> Great is our Lord and mighty in power;
> his understanding has no limit. – Psalm 147:4-5

God has determined the number of stars that exist. He knows each one intimately, meaning He knows every aspect of each one – their size, their weight, the number of atoms, the cracks on their surfaces, the time of their creation and every other detail. His knowledge is infinite.

Memorize Psalm 147:4-5

Session 2 – The Knowledge of God

In this session, we will attempt to review the things God knows. This may be an exercise in futility, for it would take more than a few pages to list what you or I know; how many pages would it take to list what God knows!? Yet, a study of the Omniscience of God would be worthless without at least trying to highlight those main areas of His knowledge.

God Knows Himself

God can only be Omniscient if He first knows that which is most important. Therefore, God must know Himself before He knows anything else.

We know ourselves pretty well and yet we always surprise ourselves. We learn things about ourselves that we never knew. God never has that experience. He knows everything about Himself. Our knowledge of ourselves is incomplete, so we are always trying to figure out who we are. God is secure in His complete knowledge of Himself.

> *For who among men knows the thoughts of a man except the spirit of the man which is in him? Even so the thoughts of God no one knows except the Spirit of God. – 1 Corinthians 2:11*

Only God knows His own thoughts. We will never fully grasp all He knows. Now we only see in part, but then we will know more fully (1 Corinthians 13:12). We will learn many things in Heaven. We will have Eternity to learn as much as we can. Yet, as long as Eternity is, we will not know everything. We will never be Omniscient, as He is. As finite beings, we will never know everything about the Infinite God.

However, although we may always have an ignorance of God, He is fully knowledgeable of Himself. Therefore, He is fully knowledgeable of the Eternal and the Infinite for that is what God is. Only God is Eternal and therefore only God knows of Eternal things and He knows them fully. Only God is Infinite and therefore only God knows of Infinite things and He knows them fully. God knows all of His attributes and knows them fully. This is what allows Him to be God.

If God did not know about His Omnipotence, He would not know what He could do and whether He could keep His promises. Therefore, He would not be able to guarantee our future inheritance. If God did not know about His Immutability, He would not know whether He would change His mind and therefore would not be able to assure us that things wouldn't change in the future. If God did not know about His Holiness, He would not know He is the highest object of worship and therefore would not be able to tell us about the reason for our being. If there were any aspect of Himself that He did not know, He would not be able to tell us with complete confidence anything concerning the future or ourselves.

Our purpose in life is to glorify God and enjoy Him forever. Yet, we can only know this if God first knows Himself. He must know that He is the highest joy, the greatest love, the most precious peace. Since He does know this about Himself, He can urge us to worship Him, know Him and abide in Him. He can do this because He knows that He is the thing of greatest value; nothing is better for us than to join in the fellowship of the Triune God.

God Knows His Creation

I had an expensive watch that was not keeping time properly. I brought it to a local repair store and a few weeks later, had my watch back. However, within a few days, I noticed it was still slow. I brought it back and they fixed it again. Once more, I recognized that the watch was still not right. A third time I brought it to them and they tried again to fix it. While I don't doubt that these jewelers have much greater knowledge and experience than I ever will, I suspect I would have had a working watch if I had brought it back to the manufacturer. After all, I do that with my car, why not with my watch? The advantage of doing this is that the original builder and designer knows these things better than anyone else and are best able to keep them running properly.

God created all things. Therefore, He knows everything about His Creation. He is the one who is holding all things together and therefore, He is the One who maintains the Universe. In order to do this, He must know about every aspect and area of His Creation.

Hence, God knows the activity of His Creation. He knows what is happening on the furthest star and He knows what is happening right here on this Earth. He knows what natural laws He has put into place and how they affect the Earth: the seasons, the rains and the natural disasters. He knows all of the natural activities of our Solar System, the Milky Way Galaxy, and the Universe.

He also knows about the activity of the creatures He has created. He knows about the plants thriving in the tropical forests and about the crops drying up in the drought. He knows the plight of the honeybee and the flight of the butterfly. He knows the call of every whale and the trail of every snail. He knows the scamper of the tiny feet of every mouse and the plod of every elephant's journey. He knows every person's movement: their daily routine, their work and their play, their accidents and incidents, their hugs and their kisses. Every activity of every living thing is known to God.

God knows the thoughts of His Creation. While the thoughts of the animals are below ours, He knows each one of them. He knows their desires and their needs. He knows their joys and their fears. Even as He knows the thoughts of every animal, He also knows the thoughts of every person. He knows our deepest longings and our most intimate loves. He knows what disgusts us and what delights us. He knows the thinking behind the words we say and the reason we keep quiet. Any thought we have, God knows.

Not only does God know everything in all of His Creation, He knows more than what He has created. If He only knew about what He created, He would not know whether He could have created something better. We have said with certainty that God created all things. However, if God only created the things He knew about, then everything in creation is all He knows.

When God began creating, He did not simply create everything that came to His mind. God decided what to create. This implies that He chose not to create certain things. However, He knows about these things. Therefore, there are things God knows about that are more than His Creation. This is true about what He has already created. It is also true of what He has yet to create. Our creative

God has so much more in store for us; more than we can think or imagine. He hasn't created them yet, but He knows about them.

EXERCISE 1

Q1: Before God can know anything else, He must know H_____________.

Q2: God urges us to worship, know and abide in Him because He knows that He is the thing of G____________ V_________.

Q3: God knows the A_______ and T_______ of everything and everyone in Creation.

Q4: God knows M_____ than what He has C__________.

God Knows the Past

God is called the Ancient of Days. He has existed from before Time began. Only God knows about reality before Time began. The idea of something existing before the first second of Time is somewhat beyond our comprehension. However, since God existed before He created Time, He alone knows what has happened since Time began and how it happened.

> *...the dead were judged from the things which were written in the books, according to their deeds. – Revelation 20:12*

God knows everything that has happened in Creation. He knows everything that has happened in each person's life. He was there when it happened. Nothing has happened that He does not know. It has been written in the books. God would judge us unfairly at the final judgment if something ever happened that He did not know about. Therefore, God must know everything that has ever happened in the past in order to be the Righteous Judge. A prerequisite for a just judgment is full knowledge of everything that has happened in any person's life.

God Knows the Present

God is Omnipresent. His presence is available in every place and His eyes see everything that happens there.

> *For He looks to the ends of the earth and sees everything under the heavens. – Job 28:24*

God sees everything happening under the heavens. He knows exactly what is happening in the supernova that is exploding in the furthest reaches of the Universe. He knows the grain of sand that went out with the last wave. He knows where the lion hides in the grass ready to pounce and where the last Giant Pandas are eating. He knows everything that is happening from the farthest reaches of the Universe to the place where you are reading this.

God knows what you are doing, what you are thinking, what you are experiencing. He knows what your neighbors, your friends and your family are doing. He knows what they are thinking. He knows the depressions that people are having and the joys they are celebrating. He knows what is going on across the globe. He knows what's happening inside every border, inside every government meeting, inside every business conference.

God Knows the Future

God is Eternal. He knows what will happen even before it happens.

> *Your eyes have seen my unformed substance;*
> *And in Your book were all written*
> *The days that were ordained for me,*
> *When as yet there was not one of them. – Psalm 139:16*

God saw King David before he was born. God saw all that you would do before you were even born. God already knows the number of days each of your great grandchildren will live, even though they have not yet lived one moment. God knows the future.

He knows what will happen with our sun and moon. He knows when the next great volcano will shake the Earth. He knows where and when the cows that will give you milk in ten years will be born. He knows when the last of the next extinct animal will die. He knows who will be the next president of the nation.

God knows all that will happen in the physical realm. He also knows all that will happen in the spiritual places. He knows when the Great White Throne Judgment will occur. He knows how the new heavens and the new earth will be renewed and what they will look like. He knows who will be citizens of the New Heaven and what they will do there. He knows there will be no more suffering in that Realm.

Nothing in the future will happen that God does not already know.

EXERCISE 2

Q1: God knows the past. Everything that has been done is recorded in His B________.

Q2: God knows the present. He knows everything you D___, T_______ and E______________.

Q3: God knows the future. He knows what will happen in the P______________ R_________ as well as the S_______________ places.

God Knows What May or May Not Happen

As mentioned in Session 1, God knows what is possible. More specifically, He knows what may or may not happen in the past, present and future.

> *"Will the men of Keilah surrender me into his hand? Will Saul come down just as Your servant has heard? O Lord God of Israel, I pray, tell Your servant." And the Lord said, "He will come down." Then David said, "Will the men of Keilah surrender me and my men into the hand of Saul?" And the Lord said, "They will surrender you." Then David and his men, about six hundred, arose and departed from Keilah, and they went wherever they could go. When it was told Saul that David had escaped from Keilah, he gave up the pursuit. – 1 Samuel 23:11-13*

Saul had found out that David was in Keilah, a city of Judah. Saul called for his men to go there to capture David. When David learned about Saul's plan, he called upon God and asked Him whether Saul would come down to capture him and God answered "yes." Then David asked if the people of the city would deliver him into Saul's hands if he stayed and God answered "yes." So David took his men and escaped the city. When Saul found out that David had left, he gave up the pursuit. Saul did not pursue David because David left Keilah. However, God knows that if David had stayed there, he would have been taken.

God knows all the possible outcomes of every decision. For each possible outcome, He knows the possible decisions that will be made next. And for each possible decision, He knows every possible outcome. This continues to Eternity. Liken this to a GrandMaster Chess player. They can see 10, 15 even 20 moves ahead. God can see 100, 1000, infinite decisions ahead. While a chess player doesn't know for certain what his opponent will do, but can only assume based on his experience, God knows exactly what will happen with each decision.

Since He knows this, He is able to determine the best time and place to make His move, or in other words, to work a miracle. He knows His plan for Eternity. He knows what brings Him the most Glory. He knows what results in the most good. He knows where things are headed and He knows the best decisions that will bring us there. Anytime a tweak needs to be made to correct the course, He is able to do it. This explains why sometimes God will perform a miracle and other times He will not.

Is There Something God Doesn't Know?

The Bible seems to mention times when God forgets our sins.

> *I, even I, am the one who wipes out your transgressions for My own sake, And I will not remember your sins. – Isaiah 43:25*

> *FOR I WILL BE MERCIFUL TO THEIR INIQUITIES, AND I WILL REMEMBER THEIR SINS NO MORE. – Hebrews 8:12*

These verses seem clear. They say that God will forget our sins. However, if God forgets our sins, wouldn't it mean that there are things in the past that He does not know?

Notice that the verses do not actually say God forgets our sins. It says He will not remember them. That seems like semantics, but it is important. Nowhere in the Bible does it say that God forgets. When we think of forgetting, we think of absentmindedness. However, not remembering is a conscious act that God is doing.

When God decides not to remember our sins, He does not forget them. They do not slip away from His knowledge. However, it means He will not hold us accountable for them. He will treat us as if we didn't do them. This is what it means to "not remember."

God forgets nothing. He has complete knowledge of the past and He knows every sin we've ever committed. If He forgot our sins, there would be things that we know of which God is ignorant. We can all remember our own sins (as well as those committed against us). If God were to forget those, we would have greater knowledge regarding sins than He would. This is illogical. God does not forget our sins. He simply decides not to hold them against us when we receive Jesus as our Lord and our Savior. Then our sins are covered by His sacrifice and God chooses not to remember them, or in other words, not to hold them against us.

CHAPTER EXERCISE

Q1: God knows all the possible O__________ of every possible D__________.

Q2: God never F__________ our sins. He simply does not R__________.

Review each Section in this Session (ex. God knows Himself, God knows His Creation). Which one has the greatest impact on your thinking about God's Omniscience? How does each Section affect the way you think of God's Knowledge? Compare your own knowledge of each Section to God's.

Session 3 – The Omniscience of Jesus

When we speak of Jesus being Omniscient, it is important that we remember the Person of Jesus. Jesus, the Second Person of the Trinity, was with God in the beginning and is God (John 1:1-3). He did not stop being God when He became Man. Therefore, He is 100-percent God and 100-percent Man. The Nature of Man was added onto His Nature of God. These two natures never mix nor blend. They are two separate natures in one person. These are the two natures of the Person of Jesus.

The Bible is clear that as a man, Jesus was just like us. Therefore, we read that Jesus increased in wisdom and there were things he didn't know.

And Jesus kept increasing in wisdom and stature, and in favor with God and men. – Luke 2:52

"But of that day and hour no one knows, not even the angels of heaven, nor the Son, but the Father alone. – Matthew 24:36

Yet, Jesus knew things that would be impossible for a man to know.

Jesus, knowing that the Father had given all things into His hands, and that He had come forth from God and was going back to God, - John 13:3

All things have been entrusted to Me by My Father. No one knows the Son except the Father, and no one knows the Father except the Son and those to whom the Son chooses to reveal Him. – Matthew 11:27

And He said to him, "Truly I say to you, today you shall be with Me in Paradise." – Luke 23:43

We harmonize these two truths by understanding the Person of Jesus. It is logical that Jesus would know the things that only God can know when we recognize the Omniscience of His God Nature. However, we can see how his knowledge would need to grow and there would be things he doesn't know when we understand that his Human Nature is like ours. The mystery isn't that Jesus' Personhood is made up of two natures. The mystery is why Jesus accesses His God Nature at some points in time and his Human Nature at other times. Though this is a mystery to us, it does not prevent us from knowing that Jesus, as God, is Omniscient.

Jesus knows our Hearts

...and all the churches will know that I am He who searches the minds and hearts; and I will give to each one of you according to your deeds. – Revelation 2:23

We have seen what a heart looks like from biology textbooks or watching our favorite medical dramas on TV. So when the Bible teaches that Jesus searches the heart, does that mean He is looking at the valves and chambers through which our blood pumps? God can see these things, but the Bible is speaking of something quite different from our biological hearts. A better understanding of this heart can be found in our saying, "the heart of the matter." The "heart of the matter" means the main part, the essential aspect. Hence, when the Bible speaks of our hearts, it is talking about the main part of our person, our innermost character, the essence of who we are.

Only God knows the heart (1 Kings 8:39). Yet the Bible teaches that Jesus knows our hearts as well (John 2:24-25; Revelation 2:19, 23). The heart is deceitful above all things and is desperately sick (Jeremiah 17:9). That Jesus, the Judge, knows our hearts should terrify those whose heart is not His. Even so, the truly repentant person can rejoice in the Omniscience of Jesus. He knows our hearts! He knows how deceitful and sick we are in the core of our being, in the essence of our character. He knows how selfish we are. He knows our lack of love. He knows our sinfulness and our desire to turn from Him. Yet, though He knew how sick, selfish, and sinful as we are, He still humbled Himself to become one of us and to take our sins upon Himself. That is something in which we can rejoice!

I suspect that if any of you knew my heart, you would put this down and never have anything to do with me again. Yet Jesus, the one who created all things, knows my heart and loves me, died for me and prepares a place for me in His Father's House. He does the same for you. Does it get any more glorious than that?

Jesus Knows our Thoughts

> *And Jesus knowing their thoughts said, "Why are you thinking evil in your hearts? – Matthew 9:4*
>
> *But He knew what they were thinking, and He said to the man with the withered hand, "Get up and come forward!" And he got up and came forward. – Luke 6:8*

Jesus knows our thoughts as well as our hearts. If the heart is the core of our essence, our thoughts are the guides that inform and lead the heart. This is why the Bible is so adamant that we transform our mind (Romans 12:2), take our thoughts captive (2 Corinthians 10:5) and think about things that are virtuous (Philippians 4:8) and eternal (Colossians 3:2).

Not one thought can exist of which Jesus doesn't know. He knows each and every thought we have. He knows our thoughts before we think them and He knows the consequence of every one of them. Since God knows the past, present and future, Jesus knows every thought we have ever had, every thought we are now thinking and every thought that will pass through our minds in the future. Not one of our thoughts will be forgotten by Him and He is aware of each one of them.

The idea that Jesus knows our thoughts can be both fearful and comforting. Fearful, because He knows the evil thoughts we consider. Comforting, because He understands the good thoughts we have even when our actions or words don't quite match. He knows what our intentions were and He loves us even when our deeds miss the mark.

EXERCISE 1

Q1: Within the Person of Jesus, it is His G_____ N_________ that is Omniscient.

Q2: Jesus knows our H_______, which is the E__________________ of who we are.

Q3: Jesus knows our T_________, past, present and future.

Jesus Knows All Men

But Jesus, on His part, was not entrusting Himself to them, for He knew all men, and because He did not need anyone to testify concerning man, for He Himself knew what was in man. – John 2:24-25

There are scientists who study primates and know everything about them. Others study insects and know exactly how they operate. Of course, many "experts" study humans and think they know all there is to know about the way we act, think and feel. However, time usually proves that their knowledge is surface level and often incomplete and incorrect. Hence, the "sciences" regarding Man are always changing. They adjust for new data and new findings. This makes sense when we remember that the term "science" means knowledge. We do not have total knowledge. Therefore, we must always update our "science" when new information is found.

The Son of God, on the other hand, does have total knowledge and He knows Man fully and intimately. He knows the way we think and what our desires and our inclinations are. He knows our nature. Therefore, He knows why we do what we do. His knowledge of us will never change because it is complete and correct. Jesus knows all men and what is in Man.

Many people think God doesn't care about us as individuals. He is too busy and has better things to do than to listen to our prayers or care about our problems. He doesn't have time to think about you and me. We're too insignificant. Maybe we count a little if we are one of the important, rich, or famous people of the world. But the rest of us aren't worth His time.

This is not what the Bible teaches. Jesus knows all men. He knows you as intimately as He knows the most powerful man in the world, the richest man in the world and the most famous man in the world. We need not worry about whether God has time for us because God is outside of Time and it doesn't affect Him. The Bible explains what Jesus thinks about you. Jesus calls you friend (John 15:14). He calls you His brother/sister (Mark 3:34). He cares so much about you that He died on the cross to take your sins upon Himself (John 3:16). He is preparing a place for you so He can be with you forever (John 14:2-3).

Jesus knows every person. He knows our desires and our needs. He knows the smallest details about our lives. This is why we can be confident when we pray. He is listening when we pray for the important things like the health of a loved one, our finances or God's will in our lives. He also hears us when we pray for the seemingly superficial things such as finding our keys, being on-time or deciding what book to read. This is why the Bible tells us we should cast our cares upon Him: this can only be useful if He actually knows our troubles and helps us in our lives, regardless of how insignificant our concerns might seem.

Jesus Knows Our Motives

… His eyes were like a flame of fire. – Revelation 1:14

The Son of God, who has eyes like a flame of fire… – Revelation 2:18

Everyone knows what "motive" is due to the abundance of criminal justice shows on television. We learn from Hollywood that it is the reason why perpetrators commit their crime and that without knowing their motives, there can be no conviction. While this is not actually true (people are convicted for their guilt, not their reasoning), motive is important. It helps the judge determine a criminal's sentence. For example, a person who killed defending a child might not receive the same sentence as someone who murdered for money. So we can understand why someone's motive would play an important part in his or her judgment.

In the verses above, we see Jesus with eyes of fire. We remember that God first related fire to Himself when He appeared to Moses as fire in the Burning Bush (Exodus 3:2) and also to the Israelites as a pillar of fire by night (Exodus 13:21-22). The Bible also identifies fire with His glory, which was like a consuming fire (Exodus 24:17). Additionally, fire is a sign of the Holy Spirit, who came upon the disciples as tongues of fire (Acts 2:3-4). However, often fire is used in the Bible to describe the judgment of God (Psalm 89:46, Lamentations 2:4, 1 Corinthians 3:13). So while we see fire representing the glory of the Father and the presence of the Spirit, it also represents the judgment by the Son.

> *...wait until the Lord comes who will both bring to light the things hidden in the darkness and disclose the motives of men's hearts... – 1 Corinthians 4:5*
>
> *For not even the Father judges anyone, but He has given all judgment to the Son – John 5:22*

Jesus will be the judge of the living and the dead (Acts 10:42). When He comes as Judge, He will bring light to all the things hidden in the darkness and will disclose the motives of men's hearts. He knows the motive of everything we have done. In His role of Judge, He will use that knowledge to compensate everyone according to their deeds. (2 Corinthians 5:10). A good judge cannot do his job properly if he does not have all the facts. In order for Jesus to judge all things, He must know all things. Jesus, as the Omniscient God, has all the facts, including the motives of every action. He will judge each person with truth and justice.

EXERCISE 2

Q1: Jesus knows the species called M_____ as well as every I____________________.

Q2: Jesus knows the S______________ D__________ of our lives.

Q3: Jesus has E_____ of F____, which represents His J_______________.

Q4: Since Jesus is a good judge, He must have all the F___________.

Jesus Knows the Father in a Distinct Way

All things have been handed over to Me by My Father; and no one knows the Son except the Father; nor does anyone know the Father except the Son, and anyone to whom the Son wills to reveal Him. – Matthew 11:27

We can read all the biographies that exist on any of our Presidents but we will still never know them like their spouse and children know them. We can know about a person by reading about them. However, there is a difference between knowing about someone and knowing them intimately by experience. Our family knows us better than anyone else does because they have gained an understanding of us through familiarity. They have seen us in ways that others haven't. They know what gives us joy and what brings pain. They understand our priorities. They can sense things about us that others miss. This is true with Jesus and the Father.

Jesus tells us that no one knows the Father except the Son. Throughout the Old Testament, God revealed Himself to the people of Israel. They saw His power and His anger. They experienced His grace and His mercy. They received His word and His teachings through the prophets. Yet on a very real level, they still never knew Him. Even after He had rescued them from the clutches of slavery in Egypt, they still did not trust Him and often desired to return to their slavery. As time passed, the nation continued to worship Him, but they did so in a way that was displeasing to Him, honoring other gods more than Him and simply going through the motions of worship. God went so far as to display Himself as the husband of a harlot, ready to receive back His wife if she would simply return (Hosea 3).

God's elect did not know Him. However, Jesus left His home in Heaven to become one of us (Philippians 2:5-7). Jesus knew the Father in a way that the Israelites never did and never could. He had existed with Him from before Time began (John 1:1). Therefore, when Jesus came to Earth, He had a knowledge of the Father that was more intimate and more reliable than any understanding that had existed before then or has existed since. Only Jesus came from Heaven, where the Father lives, and so only Jesus can tell us about Heaven and the Father.

Are There Exceptions to Jesus' Knowledge?

We've already discussed the importance of understanding the Person of Jesus and His two Natures. There are no exceptions to the Omniscience of Jesus in His God Nature. He would no longer be God if He were to be limited in His knowledge in any way, at any time. As God, Jesus is Omniscient. In His Human Nature, He was like us and needed to grow in wisdom. This is not an exception to Jesus' Omniscience. It is a definition of His two Natures.

And then I will declare to them, 'I never knew you; depart from Me, you who practice lawlessness.' – Matthew 7:23

When Jesus says, "I never knew you," it does not give evidence of a gap in His knowledge or memory. We must always strive to understand the meaning of every scripture and in this case, the meaning in no way signifies a lack in Jesus' knowledge. Jesus is simply stating His disapproval of the lawlessness of those who thought they were worthy to enter Heaven.

If we read any Scripture that seems to imply a lack of knowledge on Jesus' part, we first need to determine whether it is the God Nature or the Human Nature that seems to be ignorant. Then we must determine the actual meaning of the scripture, not what our English words seem to imply. As Jesus taught in the Sermon on the Mount, there is a difference between understanding the letter of the law and understanding the spirit of the law. Those who come to the words of God as the Pharisees did, practicing the letter of the law, will find they are unfit for Heaven (Matthew 5:20). This is the proper way to read scripture: understanding what the writer meant, not simply what he said.

Jesus Is Omniscient

In the beginning God created the heavens and the earth. – Genesis 1:1

All things came into being through Him (Jesus), and apart from Him nothing came into being that has come into being. – John 1:3

For by Him (Jesus) all things were created, both in the heavens and on earth, visible and invisible, whether thrones or dominions or rulers or authorities—all things have been created through Him and for Him. – Colossians 1:16

God created all things. Jesus created all things. As Creator, Jesus knows everything about His Creation. Nothing exists of which He does not know. Since He has made them, He knows every aspect of them.

...for God is greater than our heart and knows all things. – 1 John 3:20

Now we know that You know all things, and have no need for anyone to question You; by this we believe that You came from God." – John 16:30

in whom are hidden all the treasures of wisdom and knowledge. – Colossians 2:3

God knows all things. Jesus knows all things. Jesus has all the treasures of wisdom and knowledge. He came to this Earth and showed us who He is. While He was here, He gave us an understanding of Heaven, God and Himself.

If I told you earthly things and you do not believe, how will you believe if I tell you heavenly things? No one has ascended into heaven, but He who descended from heaven: the Son of Man. – John 3:12-13

When Jesus speaks of ascending into Heaven, He is speaking of receiving truths regarding heavenly things. He is saying no one can tell us about these things unless that person came from there. Only Jesus has descended from heaven. Only Jesus can tell us what we need to know. Only Jesus has that knowledge because only Jesus is Omniscient.

EXERCISE 3

Q1: No one knows the F_____________except the S______.

Q2: There are no E_________________ to Jesus' knowledge in the Scriptures.

Q3: Jesus is Omniscient because He is G_____.

Following is an old hymn that used to be sung in the 1800's, back when Christians sang songs that displayed the glory and attributes of God. It is called, "The Omniscience of Christ":

Jesus thou Omniscient Savior
Known to Thee is all I do
All my thoughts and words and actions
Lie before Thy piercing view

All my various imperfections
Every sin and every fear
Yes – my very secret evil
Doth before Thy Face appear

Were we to sing songs with words like this today, the Church might have a better understanding of the God who gave Himself for us.

CHAPTER EXERCISE

The music for this hymn has been lost to the past. However, you can make up your own melody. Sing the above hymn using your own tune, either aloud or to yourself. Try to memorize the words and the melody by repeating your song several times.

Session 4 – Mistakes Regarding Omniscience

Every so often, a Public Service Announcement (PSA) ad appears on television. These commercials try to help us fully grasp the impact of something we should know but for whatever reason, we haven't fully assimilated in our mind. When I was a youngster, Smokey the Bear would tell us, "Only you can prevent forest fires." Another was an Indian Chief whose tears begged us not to litter and to "Keep America beautiful." Who can forget the egg frying with the voice-over saying, "This is your brain on drugs." More recently, several anti-smoking ads have shown us the dangers of cigarette smoking.

In reality, these PSAs rarely provide us with any new information. They simply take what we already know and remind us, oftentimes with graphic images, what happens when we don't act on that knowledge. We might be insulted if we thought about the goals of these PSAs. Do they think we're stupid? Who are they to tell me what I already know? They're going to tell me how to behave? Yet, they do serve a public interest. They highlight that we often know something but act in an opposite manner. Drug-free commercials shouldn't be needed but for some reason, when we see the frying egg, it affects us.

This is true with our topic as well. We already know a great deal about the Omniscience of God. However, it is not enough to know about God's Omniscience. It must influence the way we think and live. So while we tend to say things like, "God knows everything," we act as if God needs to learn something, reason things out or discover something.

God already knows how it all turns out. He has known since the beginning of Time. He does not need to grow in knowledge for His knowledge is complete. He does not need to know something after it happens for He knows the future before it occurs. He does not need any kind of counsel from us for there is nothing we can possibly say that He does not already know. He does not deduce things or reason them out. He never discovers something new. He knew everything instantaneously before the creation of the Universe and Time.

Says the Lord, who makes these things known from long ago. – Acts 15:18

Even though we "know" God is Omniscient, our conduct often speaks otherwise. Then, our behavior cheapens God and we become poor witnesses for Him. To resolve this, we must improve our thinking about God's Omniscience and alter our actions accordingly.

For example, we believe God destroyed Sodom because He observed their behavior. When He saw their sinfulness, He decided they should not be allowed to live and spread their immorality to others. This is basic reasoning. The problem is, we don't even realize we have just diminished God's Omniscience. This thinking implies God needed to learn something, specifically, that He needed to witness their behavior to know their depravity. This is wrong. God destroyed Sodom because He knew who they were. He knew their thoughts and their hearts. He knew what would happen if they were to continue to exist.

Abraham made this mistake just prior to Sodom's destruction. He asked God if He would relent if there were fifty righteous in the city (Genesis 18:22-33). God said He would. Abraham tried to hem

God in a little more by reducing the number to forty-five, then to forty and so on until he got down to ten. Once he got down to ten, Abraham felt triumphant. He turned and headed back to his home. God continued on to Sodom to destroy it.

From God's point of view, He knew there would not be ten righteous in Sodom. He knew each of their hearts and knew their destruction was set. He knew Abraham would try to save them by bargaining down to ten righteous souls but He knew there weren't ten of them in the city. He knew Abraham's heart to save and forgive and so He would agree each time Abraham asked. He knew Abraham was wrong to try to save this city because He knew what would happen if they were not destroyed.

On the other hand, Abraham thought God didn't know the number of righteous souls in Sodom. He thought the Sodomites could behave in such a way so that when God arrived, they could be saved. He thought he was doing well getting God to agree to ten. He thought God simply needed to learn a little more about the people of Sodom to recognize they should not be destroyed. He thought God needed to discover the "real" Sodomites. He figured that God could discover the "proper" way to deal with the few bad apples.

We are often like Abraham. We "forget" that God already knows our hearts, our thoughts and everything we will do and think, now and in the future. So we bargain with God. We ask Him to delve deeper and find out more about our situation. Certainly, He'll change His mind and do what we think is right once He has found out more about our predicament. We've forgotten that our future is His past. When we think and act this way, we have mistaken His omniscience.

Following are some of the ways we make these mistakes.

Minimizing His Omniscience

Although we might know about God's Omniscience, we make the mistake of minimizing it. We dismiss His Omniscience. We recognize His knowledge of something but we don't think it is important or that there will be any consequences around it.

For example, Rob is shopping for a birthday party he is throwing for his daughter. All of their friends from church will be there. He looks to buy some snacks, drinks and the largest ice cream cake they have. When he arrives at the freezer section where the cakes are stocked, he finds one cake that is much larger than all the others are. He pulls that one out and examines it.

He notices the fine designs: the perfect piping, the pretty flower, and the colorful decorations. He also discovers that the ice cream flavor is his daughter's favorite and the cake is chocolate, which happens to be his daughter's first choice. This would be the perfect cake for her party. Rob then glances at the price and is taken aback by the cost. Twenty-seven dollars! This must be the most expensive birthday cake he had ever seen!

But it is exactly what he was looking for. He will regret it if he doesn't get it. He decides he will splurge. After all, it is his daughter's birthday. He places the cake in his shopping cart and goes to the cashier to check out. As the cashier scans each item, the price pops up on the display. Rob checks each item's cost as it beeps and appears.

When the cake is scanned, it isn't recognized. Several scans later, the cashier gives up and enters the price manually into the register. When the number comes up on the screen, Rob notices that the cashier has entered seven dollars. She misread the price and accidently entered the wrong number. Seven dollars for that cake! Suddenly the most expensive cake ever has become the best deal ever! Rob quietly pays the bill and quickly leaves the store, beaming with joy at his shopping luck. He can't wait to tell everyone at the party what a "steal" he got.

Does Rob recognize that this is stealing? Probably, but he didn't do anything illegal. He paid for the cake. He just didn't pay the amount on the tag. But that amount was ridiculously high and it probably shouldn't have been that high to begin with. He wasn't surreptitious about it. The store employee made the mistake. He didn't do anything wrong.

Rob has just committed the mistake of minimizing God's Omniscience. He knows it was wrong not to pay the full amount. He knows God desires for us to be honest. Mostly, he knows God knows what just happened. However, he doesn't think it really matters. In fact, it is so unimportant, that Rob won't even confess it before God. There's no need. God already knows what he did but God doesn't really care about it because in the big picture, it is insignificant.

Rob is wrong. God does care. It is important. God knows Rob's heart and knows that Rob recognizes his sin but has rationalized it, making it unimportant. God knew Rob would do that before Rob was born. God knows the consequences that action will have on himself, his reputation in the church, and the morality he has taught his daughter. God is Omniscient and He knows the impact of our actions over time. He knows how our behavior and our thoughts are intertwined. He desires that we do not minimize His Omniscience.

Taking Away from His Omniscience

We've just discussed minimizing God's Omniscience. Now, we will be speaking of taking away from it. In the former, it is a matter of mistaking the extent of His knowledge. In the latter, it is the case of removal from His knowledge. In the former, we know God knows but we don't think it's that important. In the latter, we think He doesn't know.

Adam and Eve ran into this faux pas. They thought there were holes in God's Omniscience. God knew Eve's heart before she picked the fruit from the tree. Eve thought He didn't know. She knew God had forbidden the fruit but she thought God wouldn't know that she had eaten it.

After sharing it with her husband, Adam realized they were indeed in trouble. Realizing they were nothing like God after they ate the fruit, Adam came up with his next best idea: let's hide from Him. Remember when you did the exact same thing when you tried to hide from your parents after you broke something? You ran into your room and hid in the closet or under the bed. Like Adam, I suspect you actually thought you might be able to hide from them forever and that they would never punish you for your mistake. When you heard, "Where are you?" (Genesis 3:9), you thought for a moment that you were going to get away with it. Then the closet door opened or the bedspread went up and you knew the gig was up. Looking back at it, you realize there was no way out and you probably would have been best served by coming clean in the first place.

Of course, mom and dad are not omniscient. Still, we mistakenly thought they wouldn't know what we did and where we were hiding. Eve committed the same mistake with God. So did Adam. We still do it today. We sin, thinking God doesn't know. We think that somehow we can hide our sin from Him. We need to stop acting like we are children hiding from our not-so-omniscient parents, who even so, knew exactly where we were. We need to quit imitating Adam and Eve, thinking God doesn't know what we are doing.

God knows our heart and He knows our actions. We cannot hide from Him. There are no limits to His knowledge. He is Omniscient. He knows all things. We cannot expect to sin and think that God does not know. Once we realize God is aware of every sin we make, we ought to "go and sin no more" (John 8:11).

Yet, even that is not enough. God knows our hearts. If we do not sin, yet desire to sin, we are like the Pharisees. Their behavior was perfect but their hearts were corrupt. Jesus was clear that unless our righteousness was greater than that of the Pharisees, we would not enter the kingdom of heaven (Matthew 5:20). We have sinful hearts. God knows them. Our only salvation is recognizing our own corruption and that only God, Jesus, can save us. This is what Jesus meant when he said, "Blessed are the poor in spirit, for theirs is the kingdom of God" (Matthew 5:3).

EXERCISE 1

Q1: There are behaviors that C____________ God in regards to His Omniscience.

Q2: Before He created the Universe and Time, God knew everything I____________________.

Q3: Two mistakes we make are M_______________ God's Omniscience and T__________ A_____ from it.

Q4: It is not enough to know about God's Omniscience. It must I_________________ the way we live.

Eve did not understand the Omniscience of God. Complete what you think her plan was: God won't know I ate the fruit. By the time He figures it out, I'll ...

Taking His Omniscience for Ourselves

Be honest. How many times have you questioned God? You wonder if He knows what He is doing. You wonder why He is doing one thing when you think He should be doing something else. Why has He allowed you to suffer? Why does He allow others to suffer? Why hasn't He destroyed all the evil in the world? The list of questions we ask about God's motives can fill a book. In fact, they do!

Hundreds of books have been written explaining the answers to these questions and others that people ask about God.

Here's the problem: when we ask these types of questions, we are taking His omniscience for ourselves. We are saying that we have a better way. We are saying that the path God has set is not the best one. We wonder why God would not choose our way, since our way makes so much more sense. In other words, we have made God less than omniscient. We think we know better than God does what would be best. We believe God has made some mistakes getting to this point. J. Vernon McGee says it this way, "This is God's universe and He does things His way. Now, you may have a better way of doing things, but you don't have a universe."

We also take His omniscience for ourselves when we make determinations about others. We think we know other people as God knows them. There is a story about a man on a bus. He had his children with him but paid no attention to them as they ran up and down, annoying the other commuters and simply not behaving in a proper manner. Even while his children irritated the passengers on the bus, their father's mind was somewhere else, completely oblivious to his children's activities. The riders stared at the father with scorn. They shook their heads at the terrible job this father had done bringing up his children.

What we don't know is that the father had just come from the hospital where his wife had taken her final breath. He was mourning the loss of his wife and the mother of his children. He was numb from all the recent activities. Now that we understand his situation, we no longer look at the children as misbehaving brats. Instead, we see poor little sons and daughters who have no mother to love and care for them. We are no longer observing an incompetent father. We realize he is a man who has lost his soul mate and must find a way to manage without her from now on.

We don't know the situations in people's lives. We cannot make determinations about people based solely on an instance of their behavior. Yet, we do this all the time. When we do, we have taken on God's omniscience for ourselves. Based on a single experience, we think we know people: what they think and why they act in a certain way. This is why "first impressions last" and "you'll never get a second chance to make a first impression." We might say it is important to know someone to get a proper impression of people, but then we make our impressions based on our first encounter. When we do this, we think we know everything about them. We do not. We are not God. We are not omniscient.

Attributing His Omniscience to Others

It would be strange to attribute the Omniscience of God to others. We know God knows all things. We would never credit people with God's knowledge. Would we?

Many people do this with the saints. They pray to them as if these saints can hear and answer these prayers. Saints are simply Christians who have passed away. They are no longer in our realm; they are in heaven. To pray silently to a saint implies that the saint can know your thoughts. To pray aloud to a saint implies that the saint has the omniscience to know which prayers can be answered and how best to answer them. To expect a saint to solve your problem gives that saint the power to affect the world as only God can. Even if we are simply asking the saint to mediate on our behalf to God, we have made that saint equal to Jesus Christ because there is only one mediator between God and men (1 Timothy 2:5).

We do the same thing with angels. We think that angels are supernatural beings who can do all things and know all things. We mistake the Biblical image of an angel for the image that man has created. They cannot read our thoughts or know what will happen in the future. Angels are created beings that do the work of God. They do nothing outside of God's will.

There are angels who do what they desire. They are called fallen angels, also known as demons. Demons are simply angels who have disobeyed God. They do not have any additional abilities or powers. Like the angels, demons cannot read our thoughts or know our futures. The epitome of the demons is the worst of them: Satan. We often place Satan at the same level as God. Some cults and religions believe that Satan and Jesus are brothers or that Satan has the potential to defeat God. Satan is nothing more than another angel who has fallen. He is the worst of them all but he still is not telepathic. He cannot divine the future.

Saints, angels and demons, including Satan, are not omniscient. They cannot do things based on omniscience and they do not know things that only God can know. Like us, they were not there when He created the universe. Only God is outside of Time and knows all things past, present and future.

This includes certain people to whom we attribute omniscience. Astrologers, magicians, sorcerers, and psychics are said to have access to the knowledge of God. Many people think as Nebuchadnezzar did, expecting these people to have the insight and information that only God has (Daniel 2:1-12). We look to palm readings, tea leaves or tarot cards to tell us what will happen in the future. We check our astrological charts and our horoscopes to determine our personality types and characteristics. We hope our dearly departed living in the spiritual realm now knows everything and can give us some information about our own futures.

No one can know our future but God. Only God is able to know our hearts and thoughts. God alone is Omniscient. No one else is.

We Desire His Omniscience for Ourselves

Not only do we often attribute God's omniscience to others but we also want it for ourselves. It is dangerous for us to desire God's omniscience. It is an inherent weakness of humans to covet this. Satan's first temptation to mankind was addressed to this.

> *The serpent said to the woman, "You surely will not die! For God knows that in the day you eat from it your eyes will be opened, and you will be like God, knowing good and evil." When the woman saw that the tree was good for food, and that it was a delight to the eyes, and that the tree was desirable to make one wise, she took from its fruit and ate; and she gave also to her husband with her, and he ate. – Genesis 3:4-6*

See what happened here: First, Satan tempted Eve with Omniscience. He said that eating the fruit would open their eyes, a sign of omniscience, and they would be like God knowing good and evil. Desiring God's knowledge is a longing that has gotten us into trouble since Man was first created.

Second, Eve allowed herself to think she could be wise like God. Third, she took the fruit and ate it with Adam.

Once Eve thought she could be omniscient with the wisdom of God, she saw the tree as "good," "a delight" and "desirable." This is how strong the temptation is for us to have the Omniscience of God. Recognize this temptation was to the perfect woman. Humans were tempted by this before the Fall, before sin entered. Satan, as a perfect angel, was tempted by this. In many ways, we see this in our secular society: we have cast away God and we depend on our own knowledge, which we believe will become omniscience over time.

Like Eve, we want to know what God knows. We also want to know why God does things, His purposes and His ways. We want to have His mind. It is not enough to desire to have the curtain pulled back so we can see what is going on in God's mind; we want to be the ones who say how things play out. We want our way to override God's ways. It is all part of our desire for God's Omniscience.

EXERCISE 2

Q1: We take Omniscience upon ourselves when we T________ we know B__________ T_______ God.

Q2: When we make D__________________ about others, we take God's Omniscience upon ourselves.

Q3: S________, A________ and D________ are not Omniscient.

Q4: Desiring God's Omniscience is an I____________ W_______________ evidenced by Satan's temptation in the Garden.

Session 5 – Takeaways

What Does This Mean?

Following are some of the lessons we learn when we understand the Omniscience of God:

God is Only-Wise. He alone knows all the possible outcomes of every action. Therefore, He alone knows the best path to get to those outcomes that are the most glorious. God has a plan. Whatever is happening in the world around us, He is guiding History in that path which is ideal. Only God is Omniscient. Therefore, only He has the wisdom to ensure we arrive at the most perfect ending.

To the only wise God, through Jesus Christ, be the glory forever. Amen. – Romans 16:27

A Judgment is Coming and God is the only Judge. Since God knows all things, including the hearts of all people, it would make sense that a Judgment is coming where all things will be made right. God would not be Just if He allowed a wicked person to escape punishment. Nor would He be Just if He allowed a good person to suffer injustice without rectifying it. Judgment must occur for all things to be made right and only someone who knows all things can judge. Only God can be a perfect and fair judge.

But God is the Judge; He puts down one and exalts another. – Psalm 75:7

And the heavens declare His righteousness, For God Himself is judge. – Psalm 50:6

For not even the Father judges anyone, but He has given all judgment to the Son – John 5:22

God is Gracious. Since God knows everything about us, He also knows our hearts. He knows our hearts are deceitful above all things and desperately wicked (Jeremiah 17:9). Yet, even as wicked as we are in the core of our being, God is Gracious. Grace is giving something that is not deserved. God has given us a way to forgiveness and reconciliation. He has given us His Son, Jesus, as a sacrifice for the forgiveness of our sins. God has given us the opportunity to approach Him, to be with Him forever and to be called His Children. That God would give us all this, despite what He knows about us, displays His amazing Grace.

The LORD is gracious and merciful; Slow to anger and great in lovingkindness. – Psalm 145:8

There will be a Resurrection of the Dead. God's Omniscience includes His knowledge of the future. God has revealed portions of that future to us in His word. Through the prophets and the Gospels, we learn about God's plan. We can know He will fulfill all His future promises since He has accomplished all His past promises. The Resurrection of Jesus is a sign to us for His plan for all Mankind. His promise of the Resurrection and Eternal Life allows us to know we will be with Him forever.

> *"I am the resurrection and the life; he who believes in Me will live even if he dies, and everyone who lives and believes in Me will never die. Do you believe this?" – John 11:25-26*

We Humble Ourselves. Recognizing the Omniscience of God emphasizes how little we know. We tend to think of ourselves as the smartest, most knowledgeable creatures in the universe. When we see the depth and breadth of God's knowledge, it humbles us. This is what Job experienced when he realized how much God knew and how small his own knowledge was.

> *Then Job answered the Lord and said, "Behold, I am insignificant; what can I reply to You? I lay my hand on my mouth. – Job 40:3-4*

We Worship Him. How can we not worship Him when we know about His Omniscience? He has seen us before we were born and known us from beginning to the end. He knows what is best for us and guides us in that way. He knows our every sin and yet still provides us a path to eternal life. All of this causes us to worship.

We Pray to Him. Praying does not give God additional knowledge. He already knows what we will pray before we have said a word. We pray to acknowledge He knows what is best for us. We confess to acknowledge He knows our sins. We praise to acknowledge His majesty. Proper prayer proves that we understand He knows our thoughts, desires and needs; that He knows what is best for us now and in the future; that He knows what is best for His glory. When we pray, we affirm our need for Him since we don't know these things ourselves.

We are Comforted. Since God is Omniscient, we can rest assured in the knowledge that God knows what is good for us and for the world; now and for eternity. This includes difficulties and offenses against us. God has known about them and allowed them because they will result in something better than had they not occurred. He knows all the possibilities of what could happen in the future and is allowing the best course to take place. He hears our cries and knows every sigh we breathe. When something is not going well for us, we can trust that He is doing something to prepare us, sharpen us, and perfect us. He knows the culmination of all things, including ourselves, and is bringing us to that grand finale. This brings comfort to His children.

A Time for Meditation

Let us spend some time thinking about the truths we have learned. Read each statement below and spend 30-seconds meditating on each. Fully reflect on each statement before going on to the next.

- God knows everything in the physical and spiritual realms - past, present and future.
- God knows everything intimately.
- He knows every possible situation that has never occurred.
- God knows Himself.
- He knows the activities and thoughts of everything and everyone in His Creation.
- God knows more than His Creation.

- God knows the Past, Present and Future.
- He knows all the possible outcomes of every possible decision.
- Jesus, as God, is omniscient.
- Jesus knows Mankind as well as every individual.
- Jesus will judge perfectly, so He must have all the facts.
- Before God created anything, He knew everything instantaneously.
- Knowing that God is Omniscient will influence the way we live.

CHAPTER 4

Omnipotence

The English word "omnipotence" comes from the Latin "omnipotens." "Omni" means "all." "Potens" means "powerful." So literally, "omnipotence" means "all-powerful." In the Bible, we read about God being "Almighty," which is a synonym for Omnipotent. The King James Version uses the word Omnipotence once, in Revelation 19:6 ("...for the Lord God omnipotent reigneth..."). Most English-version Bibles use the term "Almighty" instead. In other words, the word "Omnipotent" is used only once and only in a small number of Bibles. It is the Greek word, "Pantokrator," which is used ten times in the New Testament. Only once is it translated as Omnipotent and only in the King James and a few other versions. Everywhere else, we will see the word "Almighty." Almighty means All-powerful, or Omnipotent.

"Almighty" is used forty-eight times in the Old Testament. The word is "Shaddai" in Hebrew. Many of you might have heard the term "El Shaddai." This is the Hebrew for "Almighty God." "Almighty" is used of God alone and often it is used as a Name for God.

> *Alas for the day! For the day of the LORD is near, And it will come as destruction from the Almighty.*
> *– Joel 1:15*

God is Almighty. He can do all things. Isaiah tells us that God's arms are not too short. This means He is able to do whatever He wants. However, God doesn't actually have arms. He has no body. God is Spirit. The Bible uses anthropomorphisms to help us to know God. That means it describes God with Human attributes to help us understand Him. So how does God create or do anything without arms? He simply wills it.

Sometimes, we call it "speaking," as when we say He created the universe by speaking. God speaks only so we can hear and understand, but God does not need to speak aloud. We often speak to ourselves, but if we speak to ourselves out loud, we would probably end up in an institution. In reality, we don't actually speak to ourselves; we simply think thoughts. This is how God creates and uses His power; not by hands or arms or speech, but by thought, or better – by will. He wills something to happen and it does. He wills something to be created and it is.

He doesn't need matter to create. He can create out of nothing. A group of scientists went to God to tell Him they don't need Him anymore. "We can clone people. We can create test tube babies. We don't need you." God replied, "You do realize that cloning and in vitro fertilization require a pre-existing person to clone or to impregnate." The scientists said, "Yes, we do. But we know we can do these even without another person. When you created Adam, you made Him from the earth. We're confident we can do the same." So God said, "OK. Then let's have a contest. Let's see who can make a better Man." "You're on!" The scientists proceeded to bend down to grab some dirt, but God stopped them. "Wait!" He said. "That's mine. Go make your own dirt."

God created everything from nothing. He did it by simply willing it. He can continue to create without anything. He will form a New Heaven and Earth with features we cannot imagine. But God has not only imagined it, He has planned it and will create it because He is able. This is the Omnipotence of God.

Omnipotence is an attribute of God. It is not something He has gained or something He can lose. It is a part of Him just as our skin, our heart and our brain is a part of us. If any of these things were to be taken away, we would cease to exist. This is how it is with the attributes of God. Omnipotence is an elemental part of God and has always been. It has not come from anywhere and will not go anywhere. It was never given to Him and it can never be removed from Him.

God is Omnipotent.

Session 1 – What is the Omnipotence of God

Power – Part 1:

You enter the classroom and your teacher tells you to put your books down and stand against the wall. You do it.

You go to work and your boss tells you to go pick up his friend at the airport. You do it.

The IRS sends you a letter and tells you to send them a check for $100.00. You do it.

These are all examples of the power of authority. You do something because a power greater than yourself has told you to do it. These people are given this authority by agreement. Therefore, we see kings, dictators and presidents with the authority to rule. To a lesser degree, principals, managers and government agencies are also given this same power. When the police tell you to put your hands up or the army sends you to another country, they are exercising their power, their authority.

Power – Part 2:

In a 13-month period, Mike Tyson knocks out five contenders in under 60-seconds. You are fascinated.

Steve Jobs comes out with the iPod, the iPhone and the iPad. You are impressed.

Martin Luther King Jr. stirs an entire nation and rallies people to change the way they view race. You are invigorated.

These are all examples of the power of ability. People with certain skills can perform in powerful ways. Their abilities might be physical, such as the ability of a heavyweight fighter to land powerful blows to knock out his opponent. They might have skills of the mind, enabling one to become a great communicator, logician or technical genius. They might have relational skills, allowing one to build trust, convince people to follow or build consensus. People who have demonstrated these skills earn themselves a constituency and the power that comes with that.

Hence, authority and ability are two types of power. They do not necessarily go together. Many people have authority without having any ability. Cartoonist Scott Adams has created the epitome of this person with his Pointy-haired Boss. Dilbert's boss is inept and stupid, yet has the power to tell his much more capable employees what to do. The flipside are those who have ability without any authority. Examples of this are a prince, a prodigy or someone like Dilbert himself who has the skills to be boss but not the authority.

Yet, when these two come together, you have the textbook definition of Power. Someone with authority and ability is powerful. When you have all the authority and all the ability, you are all-powerful. When you have infinite authority and ability, you have Omnipotence. Only God is Omnipotent.

Authority

Authority is the right to control people and things. When I was a computer programmer trainee, I had no authority. I was assigned programs to write that printed forms and statements. Sometimes, a program might not print someone's name in the middle of the box: it was too far to the left or the right. My manager would tell me to fix the program so that the name printed exactly in the middle. Talk about tedious! I couldn't wait for the day that I had enough experience that those problems would go to someone else. Until then, I had no authority and was at the whim of others.

In time, I became the person who told others what work they would be doing. Some of them might hate the work I delegated to them, but now I was the one with some authority. I still had someone demanding requirements from me, but I now had others from whom I required work. I now had some power but others were still more powerful than I was. More power goes to those who are higher up in the company structure.

Authority is not only found in higher level positions of an organization or a command structure, as in businesses, schools or the military. It is also found in wealth. Since the beginning of time, the wealthy have dictated what, where, and how things would be done. When the lords of small fiefdoms had more money than they could spend at the local farmer's market, they decided to buy goods that were more exotic. Methods were needed to get these things from supplier to customer. As this trade in clothing, spices and precious gems and metals grew, only the richest could provide the ships, then railways, and later planes to move these things around the world. Power is found in wealth and this is why many people desire to be rich.

Kings, presidents and rulers are the epitome of authority. They have both rank and wealth. Hence, people have desired these positions since men have walked the Earth. And yet, even these most powerful of people have limits to their authority. Kings cannot dictate outside their kingdoms. Presidents are limited not only by geographic boundaries but also by voters who determine how long they can preside.

In other words, regardless of organizational hierarchies, command structures or wealth, authority is still limited. This is true whether one is a president of a corporation, king of a country, or the richest person on the planet.

Yet there is One who has complete authority. That One is God. He is higher in position than any king or ruler. He is King of kings and Lord of lords (Deuteronomy 10:17). God has more wealth than does the richest person on Earth (Psalm 24:1). No one is higher or wealthier than God is. No authority is greater than His is. He has all authority.

> *and he said, "O LORD, the God of our fathers, are You not God in the heavens? And are You not ruler over all the kingdoms of the nations? Power and might are in Your hand so that no one can stand against You. – 2 Chronicles 20:6*
>
> *Whatever the LORD pleases, He does, In heaven and in earth, in the seas and in all deeps. – Psalm 135:6*
>
> *But now, O Lord, you are our Father; we are the clay, and you are our potter; we are all the work of your hand. – Isaiah 64:8*

God has complete authority over all He has created. He is the potter and everything else is His clay. He has fashioned all things for His glory. As the Creator, He can make whatever He desires. Should he decide to start over or make changes, He has the authority to do so because He is the one who created it.

An artist can create a painting with a pond to the right and a child to the left. That artist, and only that artist, has the right to move the pond to the left and the child to the right. The artist is the only one with the authority over his or her own creation. With that authority, the artist can change ponds to mountains, children to birds and turn the sky red.

As Creator, God has the authority to do whatever He pleases. His realm is the heavens, the earth, and the depth of the seas. He is the ruler over all nations. He has the authority to do all He pleases throughout the entire Universe and the entire spiritual realm.

Ability

I get much pleasure from watching someone exercise great ability. I find myself staring in amazement when a professional pianist tickles the ivory. Their fingers seem to fly randomly over the keys, yet they somehow hit the exact right note for the exact amount of time, every time. It is almost magical how their hands can scurry left and right, and every stroke lands precisely to create a melodious sound.

This is true with not only musicians, but athletes, speakers, writers, and experts in all fields. People with great abilities have the power to change the world. Technologists create devices and instruments that alter the way we work and play. Politicians influence the world in positive and negative ways. Businessmen and women affect the lives of people living all over the Earth.

All of these people have an ability that gives them the power to impact the world. Yet, simply having great skill does not make one powerful. Many experts have no power. However, all powerful people are experts in something. People with great ability have the potential for great power. The powerful are those who use his or her ability to influence the world around them. People with greater abilities have greater potential for power.

There is One who is able to do all things well. God not only has the ability to do whatever He desires, He uses His ability to influence the Universe. God is the One with the greatest power.

But our God is in the heavens; He does whatever He pleases. – Psalm 115:3

Declaring the end from the beginning, And from ancient times things which have not been done, Saying, 'My purpose will be established, And I will accomplish all My good pleasure – Isaiah 46:10

In the beginning, God created the heavens and the earth – Genesis 1:1

God can do all He decides to do. God has done exactly as He has wanted since the beginning, before anything was ever created. He created the heavens and the earth and all that is in the earth. God has the ability to create all things. He displayed His power when He used that ability to create the Universe, seen and unseen. God's will was to create the Universe, so He did as He willed.

God's power is equal to His will. He can bring about whatever He wills. We might have the will to do something but never be able to accomplish it. Our will is greater than our ability. Not so with God. He can do anything He wants to do. If God wills it, it shall be done. No one else has the power to do this.

God can promise anything and we can be confident in that promise. This is the breadth of His power. God can do all He has determined. Should God decide to tell us what He is going to do, we can know that He will do it. When God reveals a promise to us, He has already willed a specific situation and outcome. We can know that the future will result in exactly the way He has said. We can trust in His promises because He has the ability to cause it to happen.

EXERCISE 1

Q1: The two types of Power are A________________ and A______________.

Q2: A______________ is the right to control P____________ and T________.

Q3: The powerful are those who use his or her A__________ to I________________ the world around them.

Q4: God's Power is E________ to His W_____.

His Power is Infinite

One of the attributes of God is His Infiniteness. This means He has no end; there is no limit to Him. The idea of being Infinite is inconceivable to us. Picture yourself stepping to the edge of the Universe. What do you see when you look past it? What do you feel when you reach out? We cannot fully imagine it but the depth and greatness of it is astonishing. Even so, this is still infinitely less than Infinite, for what we have done is to reach the end of something huge but still finite. We imagine Infinite as being a step beyond the Finite, but this is just our way of trying to think about the Infinite. Actually, the Infinite is still so much greater than that. Something that is Infinite has no end. It continues on and on without a boundary that we can approach, for when we get anywhere near what we think might be the end, we find it continues on further than we've already come.

This is what God is. He is Infinite.

Since God is Infinite, so is His power. His authority is infinite. His abilities are infinite. There is no end to His power. He can do whatever He desires without difficulty. There are no boundaries to His power. He cannot be stopped. His power is exceedingly great (Ephesians 1:19). His greatness is unsearchable (Psalm 145:3). His power is eternal (Romans 1:20), meaning His power has no beginning and no end. No limit can be placed on His power.

> *and what is the surpassing greatness of His power toward us who believe. These are in accordance with the working of the strength of His might – Ephesians 1:19*

Great is the Lord, and highly to be praised, And His greatness is unsearchable. – Psalm 145:3

Who is the King of glory? The Lord strong and mighty, The Lord mighty in battle. – Psalm 24:8

Is anything too difficult for the Lord? – Genesis 18:14

"Behold, I am the Lord, the God of all flesh; is anything too difficult for Me?" – Jeremiah 32:27

'Ah Lord God! Behold, You have made the heavens and the earth by Your great power and by Your outstretched arm! Nothing is too difficult for You, – Jeremiah 32:17

Now to Him who is able to do far more abundantly beyond all that we ask or think, according to the power that works within us, – Ephesians 3:20

"And I will be a father to you, And you shall be sons and daughters to Me," Says the Lord Almighty. – 2 Corinthians 6:18

"I am the Alpha and the Omega," says the Lord God, "who is and who was and who is to come, the Almighty." – Revelation 1:8

For nothing will be impossible with God." – Luke 1:37

And looking at them Jesus said to them, "With people this is impossible, but with God all things are possible." – Matthew 19:26

God can do more than He has done

God can do all things. Nevertheless, He can do more than He has done. That He has not yet done them does not mean that He cannot do them. It simply means that He has chosen not to do them to date. However, God could do them at any time. God will do many things that we have not yet seen or imagined.

God will punish those who have done evil, even if right now, these people seem to be getting away with their wickedness (Isaiah 13:11). God will save the Church from the hour of testing that is to come upon the whole world (Revelation 3:10). God will raise the dead back to life (1 Corinthians 15:50-58). God will create a new heaven and earth (Revelation 21:1). God will live among us on the Earth (Revelation 21:3). God will remove all our pain and suffering (Revelation 21:4). All these things God has not yet done but will do one day.

God will not only do things that He has not yet done, but He can do things that He will never do. Just because He has not or will not do them, does not mean He could not do them. Often, He withholds an action to make a point. Other times, He foregoes something because it is best.

Now then let Me alone, that My anger may burn against them and that I may destroy them; and I will make of you a great nation." – Exodus 32:10

and do not suppose that you can say to yourselves, 'We have Abraham for our father'; for I say to you that from these stones God is able to raise up children to Abraham. – Matthew 3:9

Or do you think that I cannot appeal to My Father, and He will at once put at My disposal more than twelve legions of angels? – Matthew 26:53

In Exodus 32:10, God threatens to destroy Israel and start over with Moses. Yet, God never destroyed the Israelites. In Matthew 3:9, the Pharisees are scolded for thinking they would be saved simply because they were descendants of Abraham. God could have raised up a faithful nation from stones, yet He did not. In Matthew 26:53, Jesus explains that God could send angels down to stop the crucifixion. Yet, God did not direct the angels to deliver Jesus from the cross. God could have done any of these, but He didn't. God can do more than He has done.

EXERCISE 2

Q1: God's power is I______________.

Q2: God will do many things we have not yet S_______ or I_____________.

Q3: God can do things that He will N_______ D_____.

Q4: Two reasons why God withholds from doing something is to make a P________ or because it is B________ not to do it.

We learn from the second verse of the hymn, "Joyful, Joyful, We Adore Thee," that everything we see around us are the works of God and that we can take joy in these things:

All Thy works with joy surround Thee, Earth and heaven reflect Thy rays,

Stars and angels sing around Thee, Center of unbroken praise.

Field and forest, vale and mountain, Flowery meadow, flashing sea,

Chanting bird and flowing fountain, Call us to rejoice in Thee.

CHAPTER EXERCISE

Wherever you are, look outside. Which of the works of God from the hymn do you see around you right now? Stars, Angels, Fields and their plants, Forests and their Trees, Valleys, Mountains, Meadows and their flowers, Seas and other bodies of water, Birds, Rivers or Waterfalls? Take a moment to appreciate their make-up. Then recognize God has done this and spend some time in praise and thanksgiving to Him for them.

Memorize Ephesians 3:20-21:

> *Now to Him who is able to do far more abundantly beyond all that we ask or think, according to the power that works within us, to Him be the glory in the church and in Christ Jesus to all generations forever and ever. Amen.*

Session 2 – What Omnipotence is Not

Can God create a rock so heavy that He cannot move it? Many unbelievers pose this question to try to prove there is no God. Their logic goes like this: since God is Omnipotent, He should be able to create this rock. Yet, once He creates this rock, He is no longer Omnipotent since there is something He cannot do. The seemingly intellectual question allows them to reject the Truth while pretending to have found good evidence to do so. Their problem is they misunderstand the definition of Omnipotence. They have applied a nonsense meaning to the term. However, truth is truth even if people try to spin it. God is Omnipotent. This doesn't change because people have cleverly twisted its meaning.

We've just spent the previous section understanding Omnipotence as "all-powerful." We have stated that nothing is impossible for God and that He can do all things. The truth is, there are things God cannot do. However, this doesn't make Him less than Omnipotent. It simply defines what Omnipotence means. Omnipotence is not illogical or irrational. By painting a layer of absurdity over the term, the skeptic attempts to weaken God, making Him to be less than Omnipotent. If this succeeds, God is no longer God, for He must be Omnipotent to be God.

Yet, claiming that God cannot do something does not make Him weak. C. S. Lewis says, "His Omnipotence means power to do all that is intrinsically possible, not to do the intrinsically impossible. You may attribute miracles to him, but not nonsense. This is no limit to his power." Hence, God cannot make a 4-sided triangle. He cannot make a one-sided coin. He cannot make 2+2=17. God is Omnipotent and cleverly twisting definitions does not change this.

Even the cynic recognizes this. These people mischievously smirk as they use semantics to try to trick people out of believing the Truth. Jesus ran across the same type of people during His time.

> *On that day some Sadducees (who say there is no resurrection) came to Jesus and questioned Him, asking, "Teacher, Moses said, 'If a man dies having no children, his brother as next of kin shall marry his wife, and raise up children for his brother.' Now there were seven brothers with us; and the first married and died, and having no children left his wife to his brother; so also the second, and the third, down to the seventh. Last of all, the woman died. In the resurrection, therefore, whose wife of the seven will she be? For they all had married her."*
>
> *But Jesus answered and said to them, "You are mistaken, not understanding the Scriptures nor the power of God. For in the resurrection they neither marry nor are given in marriage, but are like angels in heaven. But regarding the resurrection of the dead, have you not read what was spoken to you by God: 'I am the God of Abraham, and the God of Isaac, and the God of Jacob'? He is not the God of the dead but of the living." When the crowds heard this, they were astonished at His teaching. – Matthew 22:23-33*

The question the Sadducees asked Jesus is similar to the "unmovable rock" question disbelievers ask today: it attempts to trick people away from the truth. Notice Jesus' response: First he tells them they are mistaken; then he states they have misunderstood God's power – His Omnipotence; finally, he clarifies what is true. In this Section, we will take our lead from Jesus.

Those who question the Omnipotence of God are mistaken. They have misunderstood God's Omnipotence. They are modern day Sadducees, looking to test and fool people by their cleverly twisted dilemma. The Sadducees were foolish enough to try to trick the Son of God with word games. Jesus put them in their place. The same will happen to the unbeliever who attempts to use this tactic with God on the Day of Judgment. Meanwhile, we can clarify what is true.

EXERCISE 1

Q1: God must be Omnipotent to be G____.

Q2: Omnipotence is not I________________ or I_______________.

Q3: That God cannot do everything does not make Him L______ T_____ Omnipotent.

Q4: God is Omnipotent and C____________ T____________ the definition does not change this.

What God Cannot Do

God cannot go against His attributes. This is simple logic. A candle cannot be both lit and unlit. A person cannot be both dead and alive. A rock cannot be both movable and unmovable. In the same way, God cannot oppose what He is.

Therefore, God cannot learn since He is Omniscient and already knows everything. God cannot become better since He is already Perfect. God cannot become weak since He is Omnipotent. God cannot do evil since He is Good. God cannot break His promises since He is Faithful. God cannot go against His Word since He is True. This concept is true for every attribute of God.

Omnipotence cannot mean the ability to do illogical things. When we describe God's Omnipotence, we say, "He is all-powerful," "He can do anything," and "Nothing is impossible." Yet when we say these things, we are talking about His ability to do things that are rational and logical. Omnipotence cannot mean the ability to do something irrational or illogical. It would remove all significance from the word. In order for the word Omnipotence to have meaning, it must mean something real. The ability to do anything logical and rational, regardless of how unlikely or difficult, is the proper understanding of Omnipotent.

Examples of Things God Cannot Do

God Cannot Deny Himself

If we are faithless, He remains faithful, for He cannot deny Himself. – 2 Timothy 2:13

Even if God wanted to go against Himself and do something that would be opposed to what He is, He cannot do it. It is like trying to place similar poles of a magnet together. They repel each other. No matter how hard you might try, you cannot force those two poles to merge. God must be what He is.

Therefore, since God is faithful, He will always be faithful. If love is due, He will give love. If justice is due, He will dispense it. God is what He is. Nothing we can do will change Him. Therefore, God cannot deny Himself. He cannot be something He is not. He will not do something that goes against what He is. This does not make Him less than Omnipotent.

God Cannot Lie

in the hope of eternal life, which God, who cannot lie, promised long ages ago – Titus 1:2

so that by two unchangeable things in which it is impossible for God to lie, we who have taken refuge would have strong encouragement to take hold of the hope set before us. – Hebrews 6:18

Satan is a liar and the father of lies (John 8:44). God is Truth (John 3:33). Deception is evil but God is Good. God has commanded us not to provide false witness for it would be immoral. God is the decider of what is moral for He Himself is Moral. It is impossible and illogical for God to lie. It is something Satan and the demons do. It is something that human beings do. Lying is possible for immoral beings. However, lying goes against God's attributes of being Truth and being Moral. God cannot do something that is against His attributes, what He is. To imply that God is not omnipotent because He cannot lie is to misunderstand what Omnipotence is.

God Cannot Tempt

Let no one say when he is tempted, "I am being tempted by God"; for God cannot be tempted by evil, and He Himself does not tempt anyone. – James 1:13

The Goodness of God does not allow Him to be tempted by evil. It repulses God to see evil. It in no way seduces Him or causes Him to stumble. Nor will He use evil to cause us to stumble. God tests us in order that we might become stronger. He allows tribulation so we might become more faithful. Yet, He never tempts us, for evil is outside God's ability. He does allow temptation to come to us but He also promises a way out (1 Corinthians 10:13) and a deliverance (Matthew 6:13). Temptation is outside of the character of God.

To say God is less than Omnipotent because He cannot tempt or be tempted, would be a twisting of the term to make it mean something it does not mean. Omnipotence is not changed because God cannot do something that is against His nature.

God Cannot Sin

And one called out to another and said, "Holy, Holy, Holy, is the Lord of hosts, The whole earth is full of His glory." – Isaiah 6:3

God is Holy. By definition, this means there is no sin in Him. He is incapable of sin. It is against His attributes. God is Holy, Good and Just. Sin is opposed to these. Therefore, it is impossible for Him to sin.

God hates sin. Proverbs 6:16-19 lists several of the sins God hates: haughty eyes, a lying tongue, murder of the innocent, hearts that devise wicked plans, feet that run rapidly to evil, a false witness, and one who spreads strife among brothers.

If God sinned, He could not be Holy. It would go against His nature and attributes. He would be inconsistent in His thoughts and His actions. He would have the worst case of cognitive dissonance ever. All of these are illogical and therefore are impossible. God cannot sin, yet God is still Omnipotent.

God Cannot Counter His Will

> *And do not be conformed to this world, but be transformed by the renewing of your mind, so that you may prove what the will of God is, that which is good and acceptable and perfect. – Romans 12:2*

God's will is good and perfect. Since God Himself is Good and Perfect, His will is consistent with His Being. This is logical and rational. If God were to do something counter to His will, either His will would not have been good and perfect or He Himself would not have been Good and Perfect.

We are not speaking of the capabilities of God. We are speaking of the consistency between God's activity and His will. God may be perfectly able to do something. It may be within His power to do it. Just because He can do it, does not mean that He ever will do it. God can only do what His will determines He should do.

His will is established by His omniscience and His wisdom. Since He is Omniscient, He knows all things and so He can see the result of every thought, word and deed. Since He is All-wise, He is able to take His knowledge of all things and use that to ensure the most Perfect and Good result. God's will is determined based on this knowledge and wisdom. Since God knows what is best, He will do what is best. He cannot do anything else. Yet, this does not make Him less than Omnipotent.

God Cannot Do Anything Illogical

> *Come now, let us reason together, says the Lord... – Isaiah 1:18*

God is not absurd. He cannot do anything that is illogical. This does not mean God will only do things that make sense. God does many things that do not seem right to us. He is Omniscient and knows the positive results of negative activities. We would need to be Omniscient to understand why God has done something. We are not omniscient and so there will always be things that God does that will not make sense to us.

However, some things are actually illogical and these things God cannot do. God cannot create squares that are circles. He cannot add one to infinity. He cannot create a rock that is too heavy for Him to move, for then we are asking Him to create a movable rock that is unmovable. These are logically incongruent. They take a definition of something and try to apply the opposite. They attempt to make "A" equal "not A." Nothing can be "what it is" and the opposite of "what it is" at the same time. Omnipotence must still be logical. God is both logical and Omnipotent.

EXERCISE 2

God Cannot ______________	*Otherwise He would ____________*
a. Go against His Attributes	*1. Be unfaithful*
b. Lie	*2. Not be Good and Perfect*
c. Deny Himself	*3. Be unholy*
d. Tempt	*4. Be absurd*
e. Sin	*5. Oppose what He is*
f. Counter His Will	*6. Be evil*
g. Do anything illogical	*7. Be immoral*

Abuse of God's Power

God is Omnipotent. Yet, we often exploit God by attempting to abuse His power. We do this in two ways. The first is by not doing things we are called to do because we believe God will do it. For example, some people don't feel the need to evangelize (share the gospel with others) because only God can draw (John 6:44). Since only God can draw anyone to Himself, then we don't need to do anything. After all, the Omnipotent God is certainly powerful enough to do the work Himself.

This is an abuse of God's Omnipotence, as well as scripture. God explains that this drawing comes from being taught, hearing and learning (John 6:45). Jesus has sent us into the world to make disciples (Matthew 28:19). Romans teaches that faith comes from hearing and that people can only hear if someone tells them (Romans 10:14-17). We cannot sit around waiting for God to do the work He has called us to do. God can do it but He has chosen us to do it.

The second form of abuse is doing things assuming God will provide. We do this every time we step outside His call and ask Him to bless what we are doing. We do this when we take undue chances without reason. We cannot stand in the way of death and assume God will take care of us. We cannot run into danger and take for granted God will protect us.

Unless we know God has called us into that situation, we would be wise to take a page from Jesus' playbook. When he realized the religious leaders planned to kill him, he hid himself (John 11:53-54). David also hid from King Saul rather than kill God's anointed. The archangel Michael did not pronounce a judgment against the devil but said, "The Lord rebuke you!" (Jude 9). There are times God calls us into dangerous situations. Unless He has, we presume upon His Omnipotence.

EXERCISE 3

There are two ways that we abuse God's Power. An example for each has been given.

Activity 1: What is another example of abusing God's power by not doing things we are called to do because we believe God will do it.?

Activity 2: What is another example of abusing God's power by doing things and assuming God will provide?

CHAPTER EXERCISE

Activity 1: In your own words, define Omnipotence properly so that it cannot be twisted to mean something that God cannot do. Write it in the space below.

Activity 2: Is there anything in your life that you are not doing because you are assuming God will do it in His power.

Session 3 – Evidence of God's Omnipotence

Imagine you have just come home after dinner and a movie. You grab your keys to open the door and notice that it is ajar. Hmmm... Did you leave the door open? Did someone else open it? If someone else opened it, is it someone you know, waiting inside for you to get back home? Or is it someone you don't know? If so, is that stranger in your home right now? Are there more than one of them? Are they dangerous? Should you go in? Run away? Call 9-1-1? How should you proceed?

These questions might flash through your mind. You expected the door to be closed and locked. The open door is a piece of evidence. It tells you something is not right. It doesn't tell you what is wrong, but simply that things are not as they should be. You might have absentmindedly forgotten to close it, in which case it is no great concern. On the other hand, a dangerous intruder might be waiting inside to ambush you. Sometimes, we need multiple pieces of evidence to help us to know the full story. In our example, all we have is an open door. It is enough evidence to prove something is abnormal but not enough to conclude anything more.

If you decide to enter the home quietly and look around, you would find more evidence to help you decide what to do next. Is there anything out of place? Does everything appear untouched? Are there any unfamiliar noises? The answers to these questions would be additional evidence to help you decide what to do next. Finding your things strewn around the house would be evidence of a potential danger, causing you to turn and run so that you can call the police. Finding Uncle Freddie sitting on the sofa sipping a coffee would result in a completely different response (unless you really don't like Uncle Freddie). Having enough evidence allows us to know how to react properly.

Evidence is important as we think about the Omnipotence of God. What evidence do we have? How do we interpret that evidence? Is there any additional evidence needed for us to make a determination of how we should respond? Following are pieces of evidence that should crush any doubts regarding God's Omnipotence.

Creation

We begin with the most obvious, yet the greatest, piece of evidence regarding God's power. Everywhere we look, we see God's handiwork in Creation. We observe it when we examine the tiniest grain of sand or our tremendous Sun. We see it in a minuscule piece of dust and the enormous mountain range. We can even detect it in things made by man. Though cars, buildings and electronics have all been produced by human hands, God provided the materials to make them. Indeed, God created the person who made it.

> *For since the creation of the world His invisible attributes, His eternal power and divine nature, have been clearly seen, being understood through what has been made, so that they are without excuse. – Romans 1:20*

The eternal power of God is clearly seen through the things He has made. When we consider the Earth, we typically take for granted all those things with which we are overly familiar. So we ignore things like the dirt, the air and the water. However, even these most basic items are chocked full of evidence of God's creative power.

Think about dirt. The Earth is the only planet known to have a veneer of dirt, or soil, upon its surface. This dirt is made up of fine rock fragments containing minerals. The rock bits happen to have a negative charge. The minerals happen to have a positive charge. This creates a bond between the two. This bond is so unshakable that the only way the minerals can be released from the rock is through a chemical reaction with some type of solvent. If the solvent were too powerful, the bond would be destroyed and the minerals would be swept away by the wind or the rain. If it were too weak, the bond would persist and the mineral would remain anchored to the rock particles. The perfect solvent must be something which detaches the minerals only to a certain extent. Where would we find this solvent? It is already in the ground! It is called carbonic acid. It occurs due to the carbon dioxide in the air interacting with the water in the soil. Every plant on Earth is fed due to this. Dirt was designed by God exactly as it needed to be.

Think about air. Our atmosphere is composed of 78% nitrogen and 21% oxygen, making up 99% of our air. The final percent is a combination of mostly argon, some carbon dioxide, followed by a few other gases. Why would God have made air with this makeup? He did it because it is the perfect combination for life to exist. For instance, .039% of the air is made of carbon dioxide. Don't skip over that number: .039-percent. That's less than one-tenth of one percent. To illustrate, if someone put .039% of her $10,000 bonus check into the church offering basket, the church would get less than four dollars. Yet, as insignificant as this seems, life would cease to exist if the percentage of carbon dioxide in the air were to change just a little (i.e.: the offering was $3.00 or $5.00). If any aspect of our air were to change, just a little, all life would die. God created the air perfectly.

Think about water. Life cannot survive without it. It is the "universal solvent" and can dissolve and carry nutrients and vitamins through our bodies without destroying or changing anything so that everything remains pure. Only water is found naturally in all three physical states in the normal temperatures of the Earth. Since water becomes gas, evaporating into the air and bringing humidity, most locales do not become desert places. We have rain because the gas condenses and turns back into liquid. When the temperature drops to a certain degree, water freezes. However, it freezes from the top down, allowing seas to teem with life, even in the coldest air temperatures. Meanwhile, it won't boil in the hottest desert sun. God created this water.

Put them together and we see God's power in Creation. The water evaporates into the air. The air purifies the water. The water then falls onto the dirt as rain. The rain causes the exact right chemical reactions in the dirt that allow the minerals to be released from the rock and feeds the plants. This is only looking at the three most basic parts of the world around us. Add to this what God has done in the creation of plants, animals, birds, fish, and man. Look at what God has done on the Earth, with the mountains, the oceans, the rivers, the beaches, and the forests. See God's work in the Universe, with the Moon, the Sun, the planets, the solar systems, the stars, the galaxies. God's power is apparent in all we see. When we see His Creation, it causes us to worship Him.

> *The heavens are telling of the glory of God;*
> *And their expanse is declaring the work of His hands.*
> *Day to day pours forth speech,*
> *And night to night reveals knowledge.*

There is no speech, nor are there words;
Their voice is not heard.
Their line has gone out through all the earth,
And their utterances to the end of the world.
In them He has placed a tent for the sun,
Which is as a bridegroom coming out of his chamber;
It rejoices as a strong man to run his course.
Its rising is from one end of the heavens,
And its circuit to the other end of them;
And there is nothing hidden from its heat. – Psalm 19:1-6

By the word of the Lord the heavens were made,
And by the breath of His mouth all their host. – Psalm 33:6

EXERCISE 1

Q1: Evidence allows us to know how to R________ P_____________.

Q2: The greatest evidence regarding God's power is C_____________.

Q3: We typically take for granted familiar things like D______, A_____, and W_______, that are chocked full of evidence of God's power.

Q4: When we see His Creation, it causes us to W___________ Him.

Sustaining and Governing All Things

I am not what one might consider a good gardener. I do not have a "green thumb." A look at the plants inside and outside my home would give evidence of this. My flowering plants don't flower. My tomato plants are dying and barely have any fruit. My cactus plants are overwatered. My orchids are under-watered. Weeds are a constant battle. Brown leaves are everywhere and colors are almost non-existent.

It is not easy for me to sustain a garden. It takes an ability that I don't seem to possess, regardless of how many websites I read about the proper care of each plant I buy. The dying plants are a testimony against my powers to sustain and the weeds are a witness to the Second Law of Thermodynamics, which states that over time, everything breaks down and chaos ensues. That's the definition of my gardening skills.

The fact that everything works exactly right in the Universe is a testament that God is sustaining it. According to the Second Law of Thermodynamics, if God didn't sustain it, the Universe would soon look like my garden: dead and disordered. Yet everything works exactly as it should. The Laws of Physics continue without exception. Life is sustained on the Earth, regardless of the natural disasters that befall it. Somehow, atoms don't split, magnets have two poles, and the gravitational pull of the Sun, Earth and Moon remain at their life-giving constant.

When we speak of God sustaining all things, we must first recognize that if He were to remove His sustaining Hand, all things would begin to fall apart. We cannot take all the parts of a car, put them in a heap and wait several years until a car suddenly appears. The exact opposite is true: when we take a car and wait several years, it begins to break down. In fact, if we don't care for it, it will break down quickly. We need to keep the oil fresh, wash and wax the exterior and replace wipers, brakes and headlights. We sustain the car when we do these things. The same is true with God's Creation. If He doesn't care for it, it will quickly break down. He sustains it continuously.

> *For from Him and through Him and to Him are all things. To Him be the glory forever. – Romans 11:36*

The New Living Translation says it this way:

> *For everything comes from him and exists by his power and is intended for his glory. – NLT*

If we properly understand this passage, we learn that God is Omnipotent in a way nothing else can possibly be. We notice three aspects of God in this passage. First, everything comes **from Him**. This is a picture of His Creation, as we discussed above. Second, everything continues to exist **through Him**, or in other words, by His power. If it were not for His power, all things would begin to fall apart. Finally, everything that exists is **to Him**, or for His Glory.

The first two, "from Him" and "through Him," are about Him: what He has done and what He is doing. The last one is about us. It is about the Glory we give Him when we recognize what He is doing. He is holding all things together and should He decide to remove His Hand, everything would cease, we would die, the world would end, the Universe would dissolve. Yet, in His wisdom, He continues to sustain all things. This is cause for celebration! It is cause for praise! So we do. We praise Him for His sustaining Hand. We thank Him for upholding all things. We give Him Glory for what He has done and continues to do.

> *But by His word the present heavens and earth are being reserved for fire, kept for the day of judgment and destruction of ungodly men. – 2 Peter 3:7*

There is coming a day when God will allow all things to be renewed by fire. This day is meant for the destruction of ungodly men, not for us that believe in Jesus and are saved. Yet, that day is coming. It will come when God decides no longer to sustain the current heavens and earth and to begin afresh. Until that day, God reserves the present heavens and earth. He keeps, or in other words, guards, them until the Day of Judgment. He is God. He has already told us this Day is coming. Until then, we worship Him for sustaining the Universe.

> *"While the earth remains,*
> *Seedtime and harvest,*
> *And cold and heat,*
> *And summer and winter,*

And day and night
Shall not cease." – Genesis 8:22

All Creation will continue until that Day. God has declared it. God will sustain it.

Life

One of the most amazing things we can do as humans is to give birth to a baby. This is true whether you are the mother or the father. The birth of a child is most wondrous. As incredible as it is, the birth is only the beginning. We must then care for the child. We must feed her, change her, groom her and if she is in danger of any kind, we must protect her and preserve this most precious life. She is incapable of doing any of these things herself. She depends on us to do these things for her.

God does the same for every living thing. He gives life to the plants and the trees, the fish and the birds, from the tiniest insect to the largest mammal. He gives life to us. Yet, He does not only give us life. He also cares for us and sustains us. Giving life is not only the act of creation but it is the act of continuous care. Without that continuous care, we cease to live.

The Spirit of God has made me,
And the breath of the Almighty gives me life. – Job 33:4

When God created Adam, He breathed life into him (Genesis 2:7). To this day, God continues to give life to all who are born. God has given different ways for different species to procreate. However, only He determines to whom life is given. God has chosen to work with His creation in the bringing forth of new life. It is the job of creation to procreate. It is the job of God to give life. There is a difference between giving life and procreation. Procreation is a biological process that creates more organisms of the same kind. Yet, without God, there would be no life.

No scientist has discovered the mystery of life. Life is an essence and how it works is beyond our understanding. Frankenstein is a story of a scientist who believes he has discovered how to recreate that essence. His attempt is a horrid failure as he discovers that the "life" he created is barely a shell of what is true life. Even as this tale is fiction, we recognize that man can never create life. We can never take something that has no life and infuse the life essence into it. Frankenstein's monster was a biological mishmash. Even if we were to take a perfect biological specimen, unless the life essence is already there, we cannot recreate it. It is why science cannot bring people back from the dead. It is why unbelievers don't know what happens after death. Life is not naturalistic or materialistic. It is miraculous and supernatural. It comes from one person. Only God can give life.

for in Him we live and move and exist... - Acts 17:28

yet for us there is but one God, the Father, from whom are all things and we exist for Him; and one Lord, Jesus Christ, by whom are all things, and we exist through Him. – 1 Corinthians 8:6

Paul explains to the Athenians and the Corinthians that each of us has life due to God. Yet, it is not only that God has given us this breath of life. We continue to exist because He enables it. Our continued existence comes from the Hand of God. God has made the Universe and given it Natural

Laws to control how things work. These Natural Laws are God's workmanship that enables a consistency to life. We would not be able to perform the simplest of acts without these laws. However, these laws do not provide or support the continued existence of any individual life. People die even as these laws remain the same. People would live even if these laws were to change or disappear. These laws have been put in place by God for us but they do not determine our existence. Only God does that. Should He decide to remove His Hand, we would cease to live.

> *But, indeed, for this reason I have allowed you to remain, in order to show you My power and in order to proclaim My name through all the earth. – Exodus 9:16*

EXERCISE 2

Q1: God S_________ all things. Were He to R_________ His hand, all things would fall apart.

Q2: When we recognize His power in Creation and in Upholding all things, we bring Him G_________ .

Q3: It is the job of Creation to procreate. It is the job of God to G_______ L_______.

Q4: Not only does God breathe life into us, we C_______________ to E________ by His Hand.

Incarnation and Resurrection

We are so accustomed to living in the Natural world, that it is sometimes difficult for us to imagine the Supernatural. Yet God is in control of both. When we think about the birth of a child, we assume the natural process to produce the child. This is why the Virgin Birth is so difficult for many to believe. If a virgin were to become pregnant, it would certainly be a display of the Power of God.

> *The angel answered and said to her, "The Holy Spirit will come upon you, and the power of the Most High will overshadow you; and for that reason the holy Child shall be called the Son of God. – Luke 1:35*

Luke explains that the power of God was the means by which He would bring the Son of God into the world. When Jesus became Man, God used the natural process of pregnancy and birth to bring forth the infant king. Yet He used a supernatural process to impregnate a virgin and bring together the natures of God and Man in one person. The virgin conceiving is a display of the Power of God. The Son of God being born as a Man demonstrates of the Power of God. God's power is on exhibition in the Incarnation of Christ.

Similarly, we see the Power of God in the Resurrection. When a person dies, we understand that we will not encounter that person living again on this Earth. Yet, should a person be brought back to life after days without breath, we would know the power of God was being shown.

> *who was declared the Son of God with power by the resurrection from the dead, according to the Spirit of holiness, Jesus Christ our Lord, - Romans 1:4*

When Jesus was resurrected, he was dead for three days. When he was seen alive, God's power was on display. Only the power of God could bring life to the dead body. Only the power of God could change that body into a resurrected body, a body which was now imperishable and immortal. The Resurrection of Jesus is the single most important event in the History of Mankind for it showed the world the power of God while testifying to the Person of Christ. When the Apostles shared the Gospel throughout their world, they used the Resurrection as proof to who Jesus was and the Power of God. The Holy Spirit established and grew the Early Church through the evidence of the Resurrection and the teaching of the Apostles.

Redemption

Although God sustains our lives here on Earth, He can take it at any moment. However, when He removes us from this planet, it is not the end of our lives. Our biological life, as we currently understand it, will be gone, but our spiritual life continues. God's power is not only seen in His ability to sustain us but in His power to keep us living throughout Eternity.

Our eternal life is dependent on the power of God. It is by His authority that we are forgiven and by His cross are we given eternal life.

> *But so that you may know that the Son of Man has authority on earth to forgive sins"—He said to the paralytic, "I say to you, get up, pick up your pallet and go home." – Mark 2:10-11*

What happens when a child breaks a rule? Typically, a good parent will punish that child in some way. Perhaps a timeout or a spanking. Maybe no ice cream. Or, if the child has done something terrible, a grounding. A good parent gives a proper punishment when a child breaks a rule. Then, at the proper time, the parent will end the punishment. "Okay, you can come out of your room now." That parent is the only one who has the authority to suspend that punishment.

The paralytic was experiencing the effect of sin in the world. We live in a world that has pain and suffering, brought about by sin. All creation is now cursed, the body breaks down and death has entered. When Jesus wanted to prove his authority to forgive sins, he did so by removing the consequence of sin and enabling the paralytic to become physically whole. The curse of sin has brought upon this Earth all the pain and suffering that has ever existed. When Jesus healed the paralytic, he showed He was the one who has the authority over sin and its consequences.

> *But God will redeem my soul from the power of Sheol,*
> *For He will receive me. – Psalm 49:15*

Psalm 49 was written by the sons of Korah. Korah had desired authority and a name and so rebelled against Moses. God destroyed Korah before all the tribes of Israel. The sons of Korah learned their lesson. They understood that the purpose of life here on Earth was not to have power and fame but to grow spiritually and prepare for eternal life. Sheol is the Hebrew word for the grave, often used to mean death. In Psalm 49, the sons of Korah teach that God's power is greater than the power of Sheol. Even should we die, God's power ensures that we will not sleep. God redeems us from death and receives us to Himself.

For the word of the cross is foolishness to those who are perishing, but to us who are being saved it is the power of God. – 1 Corinthians 1:18

The cross is the place where Christ redeemed us. His shed blood on the cross is sufficient to bring the forgiveness of our sins. Paul explains that many think it is foolish to believe that we can be saved by the blood of Jesus. All other religions insist that there must be something more required of us in order to reach heaven and eternal life. We must do something, be good, and hope our good deeds hold more weight than our bad ones. Only in Christianity do we find that the way to the Father has already been laid for us. Jesus is the way. He is the Life (John 14:6). The path to God is found in Jesus' work on the cross.

Hence, those who are perishing are those who believe there must be something we need to do in order to earn eternal life. They cannot believe that the cross is the answer to redemption. It is foolishness to them. However, to Christians, it is the power of God. Christians recognize that their redemption can only come from God. They believe no one is capable of redeeming themselves. They have faith that there is someone powerful enough to save them.

The message of the cross is the power of God. The blood on the cross tells us that the Son of God gave Himself as the perfect sacrifice. The empty cross explains that He is no longer there but has risen from the grave. The symbol of the cross reminds us of His grace and mercy towards us. The lesson of the cross is that though the righteousness of God demands consequences for the sins committed against Him, the love of God demands forgiveness. The power of God is shown in the cross and all for which it stands. God has redeemed us with His outstretch arms.

With a strong hand and an outstretched arm, For His lovingkindness is everlasting. – Psalm 136:12

CHAPTER EXERCISE

What do you consider God's greatest act of power is?

Imagine what your life might be like if God had not done this. What would be different about your life and your surroundings?

We find God's power constantly on trial – "He was not able to do this," "if He was able to do that, why didn't He?" If you were God's lawyer, how would you prove His Omnipotence?

Session 4 –The Omnipotence of Jesus and the Holy Spirit

Jesus, as the Second Person of the Triune God, is Omnipotent. He emptied himself when he came down to Earth, meaning he humbled himself to become a part of His creation. This does not mean his Omnipotence was removed from him. Jesus, as God, cannot be less than Omnipotent if He is to remain God. If Jesus is not Omnipotent for a moment, then for that moment, he is not God. God cannot change and therefore, Jesus cannot become less than Omnipotent.

Jesus was the perfect Man and the Perfect God at all times. He never gave up His Deity although His Humanity may have masked His Divinity during His time on Earth. His Transfiguration on Mount Tabor exemplifies this. The veil that covered His Divinity was lifted a little for a brief moment. In that moment, His disciples caught a glimpse of His awesome majesty and they never forgot it (2 Peter 1:16-18, 1 John 1:1-2). They were eyewitnesses to His Divinity.

This gives us an understanding that though Jesus was cloaked in His Humanity while here on Earth, He was always Deity. His Deity may have been concealed but it was never put away. So in this session, we will review the Biblical evidence for the Omnipotence of Jesus.

Isaiah's Prophecies

Isaiah gave us many prophecies regarding the coming Messiah. Let's look at two examples that should be somewhat familiar to us.

For a child will be born to us, a son will be given to us;
And the government will rest on His shoulders;
And His name will be called Wonderful Counselor, Mighty God,
Eternal Father, Prince of Peace. – Isaiah 9:6

We recognize this as speaking about Jesus. The last part of the verse mentions four names that He would be called, including Mighty God. God showed Isaiah that when He came to Earth as Messiah, He would continue to be known as Mighty God. When the Son of God was born, he was born as the son of Mary, a babe, a son of Man. Yet, though he was swaddled in cloths and in Humanity, He was already, and had always been, Mighty God.

In Isaiah 40, we read:

A voice is calling,
"Clear the way for the Lord in the wilderness;
Make smooth in the desert a highway for our God. – Isaiah 40:3

Mark opens his Gospel by quoting Isaiah 40:3. He is making it clear that the straight path John the Baptist was making was to clear the way for "the Lord," "our God." Of course, Mark is equating Jesus to God. As we read further in Isaiah 40, we find:

Behold, the Lord God will come with might,
With His arm ruling for Him. – Isaiah 40:10a

Throughout Chapter 40, Isaiah proclaims the Deity of the Messiah. Messiah is coming and He is God. He "will come with might." Isaiah foresees that when Messiah came, He would continue in His Omnipotence. He would never be anything less than God, for He is God. As God, He would possess all the power of God. Isaiah saw Jesus as the Omnipotent God.

Jesus the Creator

Isaiah continues in Chapter 40 with a description of Messiah the Creator:

> *Who has measured the waters in the hollow of His hand,*
> *And marked off the heavens by the span,*
> *And calculated the dust of the earth by the measure,*
> *And weighed the mountains in a balance*
> *And the hills in a pair of scales? – Isaiah 40:12*

Isaiah pictures the Messiah as the One who Created the Earth. He sees Messiah God as a builder, measuring and marking, calculating and weighing. This is the method of the skilled craftsman creating a masterpiece. When God created the Earth, it was made perfectly. Not a drop of water was missing or a particle of dust out of place. God created a perfect Universe. The prophet of God explains that this Creator is the Messiah who would save God's people.

The Apostle John also tells us that Jesus is the Creator:

> *In the beginning was the Word, and the Word was with God, and the Word was God. He was in the beginning with God. All things came into being through Him, and apart from Him nothing came into being that has come into being. – John 1:1-3*

John, like Isaiah and Mark, recognized that Jesus was God. John explains that Jesus was with God in the beginning and that all things were created through Him. John goes so far as to point out that nothing that exists does so apart from Jesus. John's point is that Jesus has the same power that God does. He affirms that Jesus is Omnipotent.

Likewise, Paul writes about Jesus in his letter to the church at Colossae:

> *For by Him all things were created, both in the heavens and on earth, visible and invisible, whether thrones or dominions or rulers or authorities—all things have been created through Him and for Him. – Colossians 1:16*

Paul actually gives us a full understanding of Jesus' power. He uses not one but three prepositions to describe His power: By Him, through Him and for Him. Jesus was not only the Creator By whom all things exist; He was the Tool Through whom they were made and the Architect For whom they were created. Twice, Paul emphasizes that it is "All" things that have been created by Him.

Before He was born, Isaiah saw the Messiah as the Omnipotent God, creator of the Universe. After His Incarnation, the birth of God in the flesh, John and Paul confirm that Jesus Messiah is indeed the Omnipotent Creator of all things.

EXERCISE 1

Q1: Isaiah prophesies about the coming M__________ and makes it clear that He would be M________ G______.

Q2: Mark opens his Gospel with Isaiah 40 to point out that J_______ is G_____.

Q3: Isaiah recognized Messiah as C__________.

Q4: John and Paul write that Jesus created A____ T_________.

Jesus Holds All Things Together

Paul continues in his letter to the Colossians regarding the Omnipotence of Jesus. He attests not only to the Omnipotence of Christ in the creation of all things but also in the sustaining of them.

> *...in Him all things hold together. – Colossians 1:17*

The King James Version says, "in Him all things consist." These mean the same thing: Jesus is upholding all things. Through Jesus, the entire Universe is sustained. He holds all things together. He does this both naturally and supernaturally. In the natural, He uses the Laws of Nature that He created and put into place. However, one of those Laws is called the Second Law of Thermodynamics. It infers that disorder will increase and things will break down. Understanding this Law, we recognize that the Universe should result in complete chaos and all things will cease to exist. Yet they continue to exist, because Jesus also holds all things together supernaturally.

The writer of Hebrews agrees:

> *God, after He spoke long ago to the fathers in the prophets in many portions and in many ways, in these last days has spoken to us in His Son, whom He appointed heir of all things, through whom also He made the world. And He is the radiance of His glory and the exact representation of His nature, and upholds all things by the word of His power. – Hebrews 1:1-3*

The secular scientist is constantly looking for reasons why things work. However, since God has been removed from any possible answer, phenomenon exists everywhere that modern science cannot answer. How do birds and Monarch butterflies know where to migrate? What causes ball lightning? Why is the sun's corona so much hotter than the sun itself? Why are there more genes in a tomato than in a human? The list goes on. The reality is, there are things that occur in our universe that we will never understand as long as we search for only natural solutions. Once we recognize there are supernatural answers as well, we can go back to the Bible and know that it is Jesus who upholds all things.

Jesus has Power over Death

In Mark 5:22-23, we are introduced to a synagogue official named Jairus whose daughter has died. In verses 35-42, we see Jesus bring her back to life.

> *Taking the child by the hand, He said to her, "Talitha kum!" (which translated means, "Little girl, I say to you, get up!"). Immediately the girl got up and began to walk, for she was twelve years old. – Mark 5:41-42*

In Luke 7:11-17, Jesus approaches Nain only to find a funeral procession underway. When Jesus sees the widow grieving at the loss of her only son, he has compassion on her. In verses 14-15, Jesus returns him to life.

> *And He came up and touched the coffin; and the bearers came to a halt. And He said, "Young man, I say to you, arise!" The dead man sat up and began to speak. And Jesus gave him back to his mother. – Luke 7:14-15*

In John 11, we read of Lazarus, who became sick and died. Four days later, Jesus arrives. In verses 43-44, Jesus calls him out of the grave.

> *When He had said these things, He cried out with a loud voice, "Lazarus, come forth." The man who had died came forth, bound hand and foot with wrappings, and his face was wrapped around with a cloth. Jesus said to them, "Unbind him, and let him go." – John 11:43-44*

In each of these situations, a dead person is returned to life. These resurrection stories are perhaps the most awe-inspiring because we understand that when someone dies, it is too late for any kind of healing. Yet, the power of God is seen when life is returned to the dead, especially after much time has passed. If a person dies in a hospital but is brought back to life immediately, we recognize this as a close call. If a person dies and CPR resuscitates them, we thank our lucky stars. However, imagine you are a coroner in a morgue or a mortician in a funeral home. You are surrounded by dead bodies. Suddenly, one of them sits up and asks, "What just happened?"

Of course, this could never happen. Once someone is dead for days or even hours, there is no more hope of life. Yet, Jesus brought back these three people long after they had died. This proved that Jesus was a man attested by God. However, so were Elijah and Elisha, who both also brought back dead people (1 Kings 17:17–24, 2 Kings 4:18–37). So while we recognize that Elijah and Elisha were great men of God, what is it that separates Jesus from these two great Old Testament prophets? Amazingly, Jesus not only raised three different people, but he would also raise himself.

> *The Jews then said to Him, "What sign do You show us as your authority for doing these things?" Jesus answered them, "Destroy this temple, and in three days I will raise it up." The Jews then said, "It took forty-six years to build this temple, and will You raise it up in three days?" But He was speaking of the temple of His body. – John 2:18-21*
>
> *For this reason the Father loves Me, because I lay down My life so that I may take it again. No one has taken it away from Me, but I lay it down on My own initiative. I have authority to lay it down, and I have authority to take it up again. This commandment I received from My Father." – John 10:17-18*

Only Jesus has the authority, the power, to raise himself, as opposed to any other person throughout history who has been blessed to bring someone back from the dead. It is His authority. He has the power to do this. Only God has the power to give life, even to one whose life has gone and has left behind nothing but a dead corpse. Yet Jesus also has this power. Only Jesus can raise up his body after three days when his body has begun to rot and stink. Only Jesus has Resurrection power.

From this, we can know that Jesus can also raise us up again. He is the firstborn from the dead (Colossians 1:18). Yet, there will be many others who will also be resurrected as he was, making Him the firstborn and all others second. Since He has raised Himself and made Himself firstborn from the dead, we can be confident that He can and He will raise us up as well.

Jesus has All Authority

Jesus does not only have authority over death. He has All Authority.

> *All things have been handed over to Me by My Father; – Matthew 11:27*
>
> *And Jesus came up and spoke to them, saying, "All authority has been given to Me in heaven and on earth. – Matthew 28:18*

Jesus has authority over all things. He has complete authority. Nothing in heaven or on earth is excluded from His authority. We remember that authority is a type of power that comes from the rights to control people and things. Jesus has that right for he is God, the Second Person of the Trinity, the Son of God who was obedient even to death on the cross. Therefore, at His Name, every knee will bow, in heaven, on earth and under the earth and every tongue confess that He is Lord to the glory of God the Father (Philippians 2:10-11). Every person is under the authority and power of Jesus.

Jesus is not only over all people but also over all things. Every animal, fish and bird is under his authority. Jesus has power over living things as well as inanimate things. He controls the rocks, sands and hills. He rules over tornados, earthquakes and gravity. He has authority over the planets, the moons and the stars. All things, in heaven and on earth, are under His power.

EXERCISE 2

Q1: When the King James Version says, "in Him all things consist," it is saying that in Jesus, all things H_______ T_____________.

Q2: Jesus does this both N__________ through the Laws of Nature and S______________.

Q3: Though others in history have brought people back to life, only Jesus has R________________ power.

Q4: Jesus has A_____________ over all things.

The Power of the Holy Spirit in Jesus

Jesus performed many miracles on Earth. Yet, we know that He relinquished His privilege of using His Divine Attributes when He came from Heaven.

> *Christ Jesus, who, although He existed in the form of God, did not regard equality with God a thing to be grasped, but emptied Himself, taking the form of a bond-servant, and being made in the likeness of men. – Philippians 2:6-7*

Before continuing, we remember that this emptying does not mean that Jesus ceased to be God. It means that he humbled Himself. God humbling Himself to become one of His own creations is by far the greatest example of humility that can ever occur. When He did this, He chose to confine His use of His divine attributes to match the limitations of His newly added human nature. He never set aside His Deity or His Divine Attributes, He simply limited them.

So how did Jesus perform these miracles if He limited His Omnipotence to that of a Human Being? While on Earth, He does His work by the power of God.

> *"...but the Father abiding in Me does His works." – John 14:10*
>
> *"Men of Israel, listen to these words: Jesus the Nazarene, a man attested to you by God with miracles and wonders and signs which God performed through Him in your midst, just as you yourselves know" – Acts 2:22*

Does this take away from Jesus or imply He is not Omnipotent? No, not at all. It means that during his time on Earth, Jesus depended on God for the Power needed to perform the Miracles he did. To illustrate, when God performed the miracles of the 10 plagues through Moses, it did not speak to who Moses was but to who the God behind Moses was. In this same way, when Jesus performed his miracles on Earth, it was not speaking to who Jesus was but to who the God behind Jesus was.

This does not mean that Jesus does not have the Power to do this Himself. Again, to illustrate, when a perfectly capable driver allows someone to drive her to church, it does not mean she is powerless to drive herself. Instead, she has chosen to limit her own driving abilities for the time and allow someone else to do for her what she would have done herself. That God attests to Jesus by Miracles proves that He has approved of Jesus' message – that He is the Son of God and through Him is eternal life. It does not speak to any lack of power. If anything, God's confirmation of Jesus as Son of God implies Jesus is Omnipotent.

Hence, before the Incarnation and after His Ascension into Heaven, Jesus' power prophesied by Isaiah is seen in His work as Creator, in holding all things together, and in His Resurrection. Jesus has authority over all things. It is only in His work on Earth that we see him limit his power, instead allowing the Holy Spirit to work through Him. In other words, God (the Father) attests to the Deity of God (the Son) by the power of God (the Holy Spirit). It is all by God through God for God.

Jesus has Power Over Nature

While he was walking on Earth, he displayed the Power of God in many ways.

And behold, there arose a great storm on the sea, so that the boat was being covered with the waves; but Jesus Himself was asleep. Then He got up and rebuked the winds and the sea, and it became perfectly calm. – Matthew 8:24, 26

And in the fourth watch of the night He came to them, walking on the sea. – Matthew 14:25

Jesus stretched out His hand and touched him, saying, "I am willing; be cleansed." And immediately his leprosy was cleansed. – Matthew 8:3

And Jesus said to the centurion, "Go; it shall be done for you as you have believed." And the servant was healed that very moment. – Matthew 8:13

When evening came, they brought to Him many who were demon-possessed; and He cast out the spirits with a word, and healed all who were ill. – Matthew 8:16

Ordering the people to sit down on the grass, He took the five loaves and the two fish, and looking up toward heaven, He blessed the food, and breaking the loaves He gave them to the disciples, and the disciples gave them to the crowds, and they all ate and were satisfied. They picked up what was left over of the broken pieces, twelve full baskets. There were about five thousand men who ate, besides women and children. – Matthew 14:19-21

These are just some of the examples of Jesus' power over nature: He walked on water, calmed the sea, cleansed a leper, healed all types of diseases, and multiplied the five loaves of bread and two fish to feed over five thousand people.

Additionally, the Bible tells us of his cursing the fig tree so that it withered, putting a coin in a fish's mouth, turning over 100 gallons of water into wine and numerous other miracles. Yet, even with all we read about Jesus' power in the Gospels, John tells us:

And there are also many other things which Jesus did, which if they were written in detail, I suppose that even the world itself would not contain the books that would be written. – John 21:25

Jesus did these things. Yet, we remember that the Bible teaches that these things were done by God through Jesus (Acts 2:22) and that Jesus himself said that it is God abiding in him who does His work (John 14:10). Jesus explains in Matthew 12:22-32 that this power is from the Holy Spirit. After Jesus casts out a demon, the Pharisees attribute it to Satan (v24). Jesus says he casts them out by the power of the Holy Spirit and that no one who blasphemes the Holy Spirit would be forgiven.

But if I cast out demons by the Spirit of God, then the kingdom of God has come upon you. (v28)

Whoever speaks a word against the Son of Man, it shall be forgiven him; but whoever speaks against the Holy Spirit, it shall not be forgiven him, either in this age or in the age to come. (v32)

When we understand Jesus' Power, we fall to our knees and worship.

"Worthy is the Lamb that was slain to receive power and riches and wisdom and might and honor and glory and blessing." – Revelation 5:12

CHAPTER EXERCISE

Q1: When Jesus emptied Himself, it means he H____________ himself.

Q2: Jesus never set aside His D______ or His D_________ A________________ but L__________ them.

Q3: When he walked on Earth, Jesus worked through the Power of the H____ S________.

Q4: Jesus displayed his Power over N________ when he walked on water, cleansed lepers and healed diseases.

Session 5 – Takeaways

What Does This Mean?

Following are some of the lessons we learn when we understand the Omnipotence of God:

His Omnipotence causes us to worship. God is the only one who is Omnipotent. Only God is able to create from nothing, to sustain the universe, to make His entire will be done. He is above all things. His power overcomes evil and ensures a perfect future in heaven and the new Earth. Hence, we fall on our knees, lift up our hands and sing praises to Him.

Sing to God, O kingdoms of the earth,
Sing praises to the Lord, Selah.
To Him who rides upon the highest heavens, which are from ancient times;
Behold, He speaks forth with His voice, a mighty voice.
Ascribe strength to God;
His majesty is over Israel
And His strength is in the skies. – Psalm 68:32-34

We can trust in God. His Omnipotence means we can trust His word; we can trust His promises. The God who created the universe, the stars, the galaxies, and all life is more than able to give us His word without fault, without error. Therefore, we can know Him and His promises to us through His perfect word. We can trust that He will do what He said He would. We can trust in Him alone. Men cannot do whatever they desire but God does what He wills always.

I will say to the LORD, "My refuge and my fortress, My God in whom I trust!" – Psalm 91:2

We fear God because of His Omnipotence. It is right for us to fear certain things. We can fear the consequences of our actions before or after we sin; fearing before we sin causes us to live righteously, while fearing after we sin causes us to live anxiously. Fear causes us to act immediately when we see a child running with a sharp object. We should be fearful of an oncoming car. In the same way, we ought to fear God. His Omnipotence should cause us to tremble at the thought of rejecting His commands or His word. Men can only do so much to us, but only God can save us or send us to hell.

There is none like You, O Lord;
You are great, and great is Your name in might.
Who would not fear You, O King of the nations?
Indeed it is Your due!
For among all the wise men of the nations
And in all their kingdoms,
There is none like You. – Jeremiah 10:6-7

But I will warn you whom to fear: fear the One who, after He has killed, has authority to cast into hell; yes, I tell you, fear Him! – Luke 12:5

God's Omnipotence gives us confidence. We can do what is right every time. We do not need to worry that we will fail or that man will come against us. When we follow God, His mighty arm will enable us to complete His mission. God can and will do what is right, even if man should threaten us or sickness should harm us. We can have confidence in God's power to do exactly what is best.

> *I, even I, am He who comforts you.*
> *Who are you that you are afraid of man who dies*
> *And of the son of man who is made like grass,*
> *That you have forgotten the Lord your Maker,*
> *Who stretched out the heavens*
> *And laid the foundations of the earth,*
> *That you fear continually all day long because of the fury of the oppressor,*
> *As he makes ready to destroy?*
> *But where is the fury of the oppressor? – Isaiah 51:12-13*

The Omnipotence of God assures us of our salvation. God has redeemed us. We do not have to worry that we need to redeem ourselves. We can imagine we have the ability to save ourselves, but that is fairy tale. Only God has the power to save. When we place our hope in ourselves, the government, or any other man-centered solution, we will fall short. Our only assurance is in the One who has the power to do what He has said He would. Anything else is pure invention and provides nothing but a false hope. There is only one real hope.

> *Do not trust in princes,*
> *In mortal man, in whom there is no salvation.*
> *His spirit departs, he returns to the earth;*
> *In that very day his thoughts perish.*
> *How blessed is he whose help is the God of Jacob,*
> *Whose hope is in the Lord his God,*
> *Who made heaven and earth,*
> *The sea and all that is in them; – Psalm 146:3-6*

We can be strong because of His Omnipotence. We might not be able to do something in our own power. Yet, we do not have to do God's work based on our own ability or might. When we are being the righteousness of God, He will strengthen us and enable us to overcome and to perform. We do not need to worry what we will say or how we will act. We can know that when it is time to speak, God will give us what we need; when it is time to stand firm, God will provide His strong arm. Whatever we do, if God is for us, who can be against us (Romans 8:31)? This ought to give us great faith!

> *O God, You are awesome from Your sanctuary.*
> *The God of Israel Himself gives strength and power to the people.*
> *Blessed be God! – Psalm 68:35*
>
> *Finally, be strong in the Lord and in the strength of His might. – Ephesians 6:10*

His Omnipotence should humble us. C. S. Lewis calls pride, "The Great Sin." Pride caused the devil to fall and pride causes Christians to lose their witness. Everyone is affected by this sin. Yet, when we recognize the Omnipotence of God, we can begin to move from pride to humility. It is amazing how even the least of us thinks we are the greatest. We believe we know better, can do better and are smarter, kinder and wiser than everyone else is. Jesus called us to have the opposite attitude (Matthew 18:1-4). When we realize we are like the grass, here today and gone tomorrow, we ought to humble ourselves and submit ourselves to the Omnipotent God.

He it is who reduces rulers to nothing,
Who makes the judges of the earth meaningless.
Scarcely have they been planted,
Scarcely have they been sown,
Scarcely has their stock taken root in the earth,
But He merely blows on them, and they wither,
And the storm carries them away like stubble. – Isaiah 40:23-24

But the brother of humble circumstances is to glory in his high position; - James 1:9

Therefore humble yourselves under the mighty hand of God, that He may exalt you at the proper time – 1 Peter 5:6

A Time for Meditation

Let us spend some time thinking about the truths we have learned. Read each statement below and spend 30-seconds meditating on each. Fully reflect on each statement before going on to the next.

- God has complete authority since He is higher than any ruler and owns all Creation.
- God has the ability to do all He desires and He uses it to influence the Universe.
- God's power is as great as His will; He can do all He desires.
- God's power is infinite; there is no limit to His power.
- God's Omnipotence does not mean He can do the illogical or the irrational.
- God cannot go against His attributes.
- We abuse God's power when we assume He will do what He has called us to do.
- We abuse God's power when we assume He will bless us when we step out of His will.
- We see the Omnipotence of God in Creation.
- We see God's Omnipotence in His sustaining and governing all things.
- The existence of Life is evidence of God's Omnipotence.
- God's Omnipotence was on display in the Incarnation and Resurrection of Jesus.
- Our redemption is proof of God's Omnipotence.
- The Omnipotence of Jesus is seen in His part in Creation.
- The Omnipotence of Jesus is seen in His part in holding all things together.
- The Omnipotence of Jesus is seen in His power over death.

- Jesus has all authority.
- Jesus has power over nature.

Exercise Answers

Session 1

Exercise 1

Q1: Our Definition of Holy will determine what our living looks like

Q4: The way we think about Holiness will influence how we think about God. For example, if Angel is right, we may think of God as being all warm and fuzzy but without justice and wrath. If Heath is right, we may think of God as Savior but not as a personal and caring God. If Lawrence is right, we may think of God as a punishing rule-keeper and not gracious and merciful.

Exercise 2

Q1: A Holy Life is an Obedient Life

Q2: The only way we will see the Lord is by living a Holy Life

Q3: If we are abiding in Him, we are walking the same way Jesus Walked

Session 2

Exercise 1

Q1: When man creates the moral standards, that standard will inevitably Change.

Q2: God determines what is Morally Acceptable.

Q3: In order to understand evil in the world, we must separate our Intellect from our Emotions.

Q4: God knows the beginning from the end and causes All Things to work together for good.

Chapter Exercise

Q1: Only God is morally perfect and therefore able to determine what is moral. Without God, any standard is biased and may be wrong.

Q2: Moral Perfection means God is perfect and He is morally right. This means God is sinless and good. Therefore, even where evil exists, God is working out a perfect and good ending.

Q3: Jesus was sinless. In order to be Savior, he must be morally perfect. If he had committed a sin, he would no longer be qualified to be the Savior and we would all still be in our sins.

Q4: God is Triune. All three Persons must be morally perfect if God is to be morally perfect. Since God is morally perfect, all three Persons of the Godhead must be morally perfect.

Session 3

Exercise 1

Q1: God's Holiness is not only about His Moral Perfection, but especially about His Separateness

Q2: To be Holy is to be set apart. God's separateness is not simply that He is set apart but that He is "Other."

Q3: Holiness is God's overarching Attribute. Every other Attribute is connected to and subservient to His Holiness.

Exercise 2

Q1: The idea of God's holiness is at once Understandable and Elusive.

Q2: When we begin to understand God's holiness and His otherness, Worship will be all we can do.

Q3: Based on Revelation 4-5, he will most probably fall to his knees. It is what every creature does on that day before the Throne of God in the presence of His holiness.

Chapter Exercise

Q1: In other religions, a holy god is Feared.

Q2: In Christianity, we grow Deeper in Relationship with Him.

Session 4

Chapter Exercise

Q1: No one is Morally Perfect but God still calls us to be Holy as He is Holy.

Q2: Separateness from the world does not mean Isolation from it.

Q3: Jesus died for the Church so she could be Holy and Blameless.

Session 1

Exercise 1

Q1: Something that is Immutable is Unable to Change.

Q2: There can be no Change without Time.

Q3: God is Outside of Time because He Created it.

Q4: The foundation of Process Theology is wrong because it misunderstands that God cannot Change since He is outside of Time.

Chapter Exercise

Q1: The Name God calls Himself is I AM.

Q2: God will be called I AM in every Generation.

Q3: The two aspects of God which are immutable are His Person and His Will.

Session 2

Exercise 1

Q1: There is no Fickleness with God.

Q2: God can only be God if He is Perfect.

Q3: If God changed for the Better, He must not have been Perfect.

Exercise 2

Q1: God's attributes are Essential to His Being.

Q2: If an attribute of God were to change, He would no long be God.

Q3: God's Faithfulness is Great. There is no Shadow of Turning with Him.

Q4: God cannot Gain knowledge, for He already knows all that can be known.

Chapter Exercise

The point of the exercise is to help explain how God can never make the wrong decision. It should help us to see why God never has to change His mind.

Session 3

Exercise 1

Q1: God's Word never changes.

Q2: We can believe that the Bible is True.

Q3: Since the Bible is true, we can Know God.

Q4: God Revealed Himself in the Bible.

Exercise 2

Q1: We can be Confident that God will do what He promised.

Q2: God's Knowledge is complete. Nothing can happen to make Him break His promise.

Q3: God is All-Powerful. He will complete what He started.

Q4: When God makes a plan, nothing can cause Him to Veer off course.

Session 4

Exercise 1

Q1: The Gospels of Mark and John both begin with the clear statement that Jesus is God.

Q2: Those who say Jesus never said he was God are Mistaken.

Q3: The religious leaders tried to kill Jesus because he made himself Equal to God.

Q4: The Sanhedrin found Jesus guilty of Blasphemy and had him crucified because he said he was the Son of God and the Son of Man.

Exercise 2

Q1: Jesus Existed in the Form of God

Q2: Although Jesus Emptied Himself and became Man, He remained God.

Q3: His natures of God and Man never Mixed together.

Q4: The evidence that Jesus was both God and Man is found in his Resurrection.

Session 1

Exercise 1

Q1: The world believes only in the Natural but we know the Supernatural is real as well.

Q2: The four aspects that make up reality are the things in Heaven, on Earth, and the Visible as well as the Invisible.

Q3: That God knows everything's name means that He knows them Intimately.

Exercise 2

Q1: God knows about things that are Nonexistent as well as things that exist.

Q2: Things and Actions are two categories of the Possible of which we can know God has complete knowledge.

Q3: God would have created something that currently doesn't exist if He knew that it would make things for the Best in eternity or brought Him more Glory.

Q4: For God to be Omniscient, He must know everything that is Possible.

Session 2

Exercise 1

Q1: Before God can know anything else, He must know Himself.

Q2: God urges us to worship, know and abide in Him because He knows that He is the thing of Greatest Value.

Q3: God knows the Activity and Thoughts of everything and everyone in Creation.

Q4: God knows More than what He has Created.

Exercise 2

Q1: God knows the past. Everything that has been done is recorded in His Book.

Q2: God knows the present. He knows everything you Do, Think and Experience.

Q3: God knows the future. He knows what will happen in the Physical Realm as well as the Spiritual places.

Chapter Exercise

Q1: God knows all the possible Outcome of every possible Decision.

Q2: God never Forgets our sins. He simply does not Remember.

Session 3

Exercise 1

Q1: Within the Person of Jesus, it is His God Nature that is Omniscient.

Q2: Jesus knows our Heart, which is the Essence of who we are.

Q3: Jesus knows our Thoughts, past, present and future.

Exercise 2

Q1: Jesus knows the species called Man as well as every Individual.

Q2: Jesus knows the Smallest Detail of our lives.

Q3: Jesus has Eyes of Fire, which represents His Judgment.

Q4: Since Jesus is a good judge, He must have all the Facts.

Exercise 3

Q1: No one knows the Father except the Son.

Q2: There are no Exceptions to Jesus' knowledge in the Scriptures.

Q3: Jesus is Omniscient because He is God.

Session 4

Exercise 1

Q1: There are behaviors that Cheapen God in regards to His Omniscience.

Q2: Before He created the Universe and Time, God knew everything Instantaneously.

Q3: Two mistakes we make are Minimizing God's Omniscience and Taking Away from it.

Q4: It is not enough to know about God's Omniscience. It must Influence the way we live.

The goal of this exercise was to try to understand Eve's thinking so that we can realize how insufficiently we think about God's Omniscience. Regardless of the plan you came up with, it must have a hole in God's knowledge for it to be successful. Eve must have thought God would be ignorant of some part of her plan for her to have attempted it. Had she realized God knew her heart and her thoughts and therefore her plans, she would never have eaten the fruit. She would have known there was no way for her to overcome God successfully.

Exercise 2

Q1: We take Omniscience upon ourselves when we Think we know Better Than God.

Q2: When we make Determinations about others, we take God's Omniscience upon ourselves.

Q3: Saints, Angels and Demons are not Omniscient.

Q4: Desiring God's Omniscience is an Inherent Weakness evidenced by Satan's temptation in the Garden.

Session 1

Exercise 1

Q1: The two types of Power are Authority and Ability.

Q2: Authority is the right to control People and Things.

Q3: The powerful are those who use his or her Abilities to Influence the world around them.

Q4: God's Power is Equal to His Will.

Exercise 2

Q1: God's power is Infinite.

Q2: God will do many things we have not yet Seen or Imagine.

Q3: God can do things that He will Never Do

Q4: Two reasons why God withholds from doing something is to make a Point or because it is Better not to do it.

Session 2

Exercise 1

Q1: God must be Omnipotent to be God.

Q2: Omnipotence is not Illogical or Irrational.

Q3: That God cannot do everything does not make Him Less Than Omnipotent.

Q4: God is Omnipotent and Cleverly Twisting the definition does not change this.

Exercise 2

a-5; b-7; c-1; d-6; e-3; f-2; g-4

Session 3

Exercise 1

Q1: Evidence allows us to know how to React Properly.

Q2: The greatest evidence regarding God's power is Creation.

Q3: We typically take for granted familiar things like Dirt, Air, and Water, that are chocked full of evidence of God's power.

Q4: When we see His Creation, it causes us to Worship Him.

Exercise 2

Q1: God Sustains all things. Were He to Remove His hand, all things would fall apart.

Q2: When we recognize His power in Creation and in Upholding all things, we bring Him Glory.

Q3: It is the job of Creation to procreate. It is the job of God to Give Life.

Q4: Not only does God breathe life into us, we Continue to Exist by His Hand.

Session 4

Exercise 1

Q1: Isaiah prophesies about the coming Messiah and makes it clear that He would be Mighty God.

Q2: Mark opens his Gospel with Isaiah 40 to point out that Jesus is God.

Q3: Isaiah recognized Messiah as Creator.

Q4: John and Paul write that Jesus created All Things.

Exercise 2

Q1: When the King James Version says, "in Him all things consist," it is saying that in Jesus, all things Holds Together.

Q2: Jesus does this both Naturally through the Laws of Nature and Supernaturally.

Q3: Though others in history have brought people back to life, only Jesus has Resurrection power.

Q4: Jesus has Authority over all things.

Chapter Exercise

Q1: When Jesus emptied Himself, it means he Humbled himself.

Q2: Jesus never set aside His Deity or His Divine Attributes but Limited them.

Q3: When he walked on Earth, Jesus worked through the Power of the Holy Spirit.

Q4: Jesus displayed his Power over Nature when he walked on water, cleansed lepers and healed diseases.

LEAVE A REVIEW
AT AMAZON.COM
THX!
D

ABOUT THE AUTHOR

I am a former church planter and was lead pastor at The Ark Church on Long Island for over a decade. God called my wife and me to a new mission field in Florida where we served student pilots from around the world, specifically the Muslim and Atheist nations of Bangladesh, Kazakhstan and China in order to share life and the Gospel.

Today, I spend my days studying and writing.

My weekly post can be found at my website: *http://davidtue.com/blog*

I encourage you to contact me at
david@davidtue.com
to let me know your thoughts about this study or how it has affected your life.

Made in the USA
Middletown, DE
30 January 2017